http://www.fast-print.net/bookshop

My Life in the CIU

A catalogue record for this book is available from the British Library

ISBN 978-178456-564-0

First Published 2018 by
Fast-Print Publishing
of Peterborough, England.

Printed and bound in England by www.printondemand-worldwide.com

Contents

Early Days at School and Work in Clubs

Wolverton Central Club was founded in 1905 by a group of young men who had been regularly disciplined and suspended from their membership at the original Working Men's Social club in Stratford Road. They resolved to form another club and rented a house in Bedford Street with a clear understanding that they would never take disciplinary action against one another. At that time any twenty-five men and I suppose women were permitted to create and establish a private members club and supply intoxicants by payment of five shillings per year to the clerk to the local justices. So, Wolverton Central Club was created by some two dozen men, my father Thomas Henry Dormer being one of them.

Two years later in 1907 a magnificent building was constructed in a field at the end of Western Road; one needed to go through a five-barred gate to get to it; but it retained its name Central. This club was not far from 106 Jersey Road where I was born in 1926, the tenth of a family of twelve children, seven boys and five girls and we lived above and behind the Co-operative butchers shop.

Life in those days in the Twenties and Thirties revolved around Wolverton railway carriage works, McCorquodale printers, the Co-operative Society and the Working Men's Clubs. Virtually every male over the age of twenty-one was a member of one or the other of these clubs, sometimes both.

Other than children who had no siblings or were the offspring of professional people, most youngsters were brought up in quite serious poverty. There were of course, six churches in the town of various denominations, which gave some relief and pleasure from time to time to the congregations. Children looked forward to the Working Men's Clubs annual treat which took the form of a trip to Whipsnade Zoo or Wicksteed Park or a tea party given by the church or chapel which everybody attended on Sunday mornings or afternoon.

In working-class areas such as Wolverton at that time a vital part of men's lifestyle was membership of one of the Working Men's Clubs. It was not possible to enrol as a member under the age of twenty-one. This coincided with many hundreds and thousands of young men finishing their apprenticeships. Nearly all social life revolved around activity and attendance at the clubs. At the same time each of the six churches provided recreation facilities for the younger element of the male population from fourteen onwards and it was in these church clubs that men began to learn the art of billiards, snooker, darts, card games and so on.

I was born in the middle of the General Strike in 1926. Mother told the story of the occasion when I was a day or two old in her arms and the Strike Committee brought a ten shillings note around, she had the money in one hand and me on the other and she didn't know which was most valuable!

One reason no doubt for the Strike Committees' benevolence was that I already had five brothers and four sisters at that time with another brother and sister to follow, making twelve children in all.

Despite father having a reputation in some quarters like many working men of often being drunk, I think the twelve children proves he could not have been inebriated all the time. One thing was certain we were very poor. Some of the older siblings were at work and contributed to the household and it stood to reason that they were also building nest eggs to be sure they could fly this overcrowded nest at the earliest opportunity. All these siblings seven boys and five girls with a couple of exceptions were prominent in sports particularly football, cricket swimming and running. All the boys with one exception passed the medical and worked in the railway workshop and three of the girls were employed in the sweat-shops of McCorquodale Printers.

My early memory goes back to when I was probably three years of age and used to enjoy blocking up gutters in order to create ponds. My happiest memory was when I was five years of age and was told I could go to school. When the day came; off I went and presented myself to a teacher, I was put in a class and the first lesson was she taught us to write our name. I could already do that and I was somewhat mystified that there was so little to learn.

A year later now six years old, I well remember having a raging toothache. It was decided that when Friday came I would be allowed to make a collection around the tea-table for half a crown the cost, of the dentist. My eldest sister Ethel had promised to contribute sixpence if I collected the balance of two shillings. I went around the table with my grubby little hands and managed to raise the necessary two shillings. It was now six o'clock in the evening in the winter and I walked alone to Ethel's house which was the last one in the town of Wolverton with my hands full of these coppers. She then took me to the dentist, Mr. Montague Watts.

It was not unusual for doctors and dentists to work throughout the evening until perhaps eight or nine o'clock. When they sat me in his chair he said immediately there is an abscess under his tooth and I cannot possibly take it out for half crown. It would need gas and that was ten shillings.

As this was going on another man was putting his top coat and hat on whom I later realised was the doctor who had to be present for a gas extraction for an earlier patient. He had no intention of doing it for nothing so we left the surgery and I gave back the contributions to those who had made them.

By a stroke of good fortune, after the weekend a school dentist came to check which children needed treatment. Everyone had been checked by eleven thirty when the Headmistress came into the class whispered to the teacher, she called me to them and explained that my tooth had to be removed that day although the treatments were not scheduled at that time. I was asked to bring my mother to the school in the afternoon. I explained that she would not be able to come simply because I thought she would not want to. It was decided therefore that the dentist would remove the tooth there and then. I was sat in the chair watched by the nurse, my teacher and the Headmistress while this operation took place. I was somewhat bewildered why there was so much fuss being made and was conveyed to a tiny chair. The nurse and my teacher who were both crying went off to prepare some warm milk. Twelve o'clock arrived and somebody remembered I had an elder sister Eileen upstairs in what was known as the big girl's school, she was located with the instruction to take me home. She wanted to know why they gave me the warm milk and then ran off. My mother explained that had she known she would have come to school. We didn't pay the shilling. There is no doubt that I was, if not before then certainly after that event the teacher's little pet and darling.

One day Miss Skinner the Headmistress and Miss Jones my teacher told me to wait behind after school, they said that somebody had left a coat in the cloakroom and as they could not find the owner they were going to give it to me. This was a story because they had obviously purchased the coat (these two ladies lived together) I was six then and I wore the same coat until I was nearly nine.

At eight years of age I moved to the big boy's school which was in the next road. They had a lady teacher Miss James with a reputation for being severe with the new intake of big boys. I was quite fearful of her but soon became her star pupil. However like Miss Fry in the infants school, she still had a prejudice towards the boys and girls who attended her church usually if their fathers had served in India in the Forces where I imagined she had been born. Miss James was the same, or I may have excelled even more so.

At this time I was eight going on nine years of age I had never had a holiday and arrangements were made for us to go to Ramsgate where my mother had a sister Frances. The travel was free for railway people and the journey was horrendous. My mother with five or six children barely properly dressed began the journey early on Saturday morning. When we reached Victoria Station in London my father disappeared and left his brood with mother on the concourse and came back several hours later well inebriated. None of us had any refreshment but we were still, after the long wait, excited at the prospect of seeing the seaside for the first time.

I had never had a bathing costume but the next day early after breakfast in order to fulfil a long held dream of playing and perhaps swimming in the sea, together with two brothers and two sisters we went to the beach, removed our pathetic clothing, donned the costumes, mine of course being a gift from a relative or charity organisation and dashed excitedly to the waters edge. As we entered the water, and I was immersed to my chest the costume had dissolved. The realisation of my situation was at the same time traumatic, frustrating, disappointing, and bewildering all of those emotions became worse as my dilemma deepened. For a nine year old boy to be naked in public was unthinkable, the sea was in front I turned round with the great cliffs behind me and my little heap of clothing some fifty yards away. There were not many options, somehow I got to the clothes and what was called a towel, dried, dressed, and never went in again.

That day news came that my mother's mother had died and we were to go back early before the week was out and when we got home her father had died as well.

In 1936, Buckinghamshire County Council began research into IQ tests known then as intelligence tests which were later introduced as preliminary to the Eleven Plus. On the first occasion they were tested in our school, Richard Riddell an only child and a friend of mine and myself both secured one hundred percent. When these results were studied they obviously revealed a weakness in the tests and at the same time the authorities concerned found it difficult to believe. A couple of weeks later we were segregated and taken off to do another intelligence test under different supervision. Richard again got one hundred percent and I got ninety-eight. A couple of years later the tests were introduced into all Eleven Plus examinations. The following year we took what was the fore-runner of the Eleven Plus which at that time was called the scholarship. The idea was that fifty boys and girls from North Bucks were to be given places at the County Secondary School, later to be known as the Grammar School. When the results were announced in competitive order Richard Riddell came top and I came about ninth.

One winter Saturday later that year, I went out to play. When I went home at dinner time there was nobody in the house so I did not have any dinner and went out to play again. When I came back at teatime there were no lights on and no one in the house, no fire, no food, no-one and I had no idea where anybody was. Eventually about eight o'clock my brother Reg arrived with his girlfriend Dorothy, they were about eighteen years old. Reg realised the situation and explained to me that the family, mother and father had all gone to London to visit my sister Olive who had recently married. Dorothy was rather anxious to leave and Reg, I felt was somewhat reluctant. However he said the family would be back at ten and I had to agree with that. I then decided about eight thirty to walk to the station to meet them off the London train it was about a two mile walk. Nearing the station in a lonely part of Wolverton I was accosted by three youths from Bradwell one a lad called Alan White. They said they knew me and decided they were going to beat me up as they put it. I could not have defended myself against Alan White so in a pathetic attempt to save my skin I offered them all I had in the world which was one penny to let me go. Believing even at their youthful age it would be criminal to take my money and in the goodness of his heart he let me go.

When I got to the station it was dark, for several hours my anxiety had been growing coupled with that I was still in shock from the threatened beating. I did not feel confident enough to ask an official whether any trains were due or had recently arrived from London. Therefore I decided to walk back in the hope that whilst walking they would have passed me in the bus. I got home around nine forty-five and the house was still deserted so I felt there was nothing to do but sit it out. Eventually around ten I heard laughter and joyful voices coming to the door. The men folk had dropped off at the club and the women and children came in after a good day out. I was given a candle to light my way to bed and that was the end of the day. Since breakfast no food, no drink, no heat, and no explanation.

When I was eleven and the results of the Scholarship were announced the Headmaster Mr. Herbert Lunn was highly delighted with our performance Eight boys in all from the school had been awarded the Scholarship and he presented us with a package containing the details to take home at Friday mid-day. I was quite excited and a little proud. My mother stood talking to the next door neighbour and I showed the package to her saying I have won the Scholarship and she said, "You won't go". The next day a letter arrived for my mother and father from the House of Commons containing local MPs congratulations upon my success. As the MP was a Conservative my father tore up the letter and threw it on the fire. In the event I think through pressure of my elder siblings it was agreed that I could take up the Scholarship. The main problems being that the cost of the bare necessities and clothing was approximately one pound five shillings. It also meant that I would not be starting work at fourteen as the leaving age from Grammar School was nearer to seventeen.

Wolverton was a vibrant district, notwithstanding the struggle which many parents had to feed and clothe their children but the enthusiasm to overcome the problems was enormous.

Education was a serious and vital pursuit for working people in those days. At eight years of age children became big boys and big girls and were split into different schools. Big boys were in another building and big girls went upstairs in the Infants building. At thirteen some went to either the Technical College for two years, to learn Mechanical Drawing, Metalwork and the like and others particularly the girls went to the Commercial College to study shorthand, typing, commercial English and Maths. At fifteen they left the schools but the majority of children had finished their education at the age of fourteen.

However such was the desire for learning and training that most children resorted to evening classes held mainly at the Technical and Commercial colleges. There courses were held for boys to obtain the National Certificate in trades running parallel with their apprenticeships in the railway works or obtain qualification from the Royal Society of Arts in Shorthand and Typing and other office skills.

I had always enjoyed school and beginning a new phase at what was then effectively Wolverton Grammar School I found the experience a great pleasure and very exciting and in the first years did extremely well with my studies. With the onset of the war half way through my five year course the difficulty of keeping up with the money required at school determined that I would need to work part-time. So at thirteen I obtained a job working for a greengrocer at the market after school on Friday and all day Saturday.

This produced half crown in payment which when added to my newspaper delivery wages of nine pence on Sunday meant that I was reasonably well off. One of the necessities which I had been denied was a bicycle and in 1939 I sought to purchase a machine through a catalogue with repayments amounting to six shillings and six pence each month for eighteen months and this I was quite capable of earning. In 1940 my Father had his first heart attack and was not able to work and from then on I found it incumbent upon me to pay two shillings a week to him so that he could obtain some beer on Saturday nights.

Throughout this time indeed since I had been ten my brother Jack who had suffered from rheumatic fever as a boy and therefore had a faulty heart had decided it would be unfair to take a wife. He therefore had a little surplus cash from his earnings and as he played the violin he took it upon himself to provide me with piano lessons twice a week. Although I was not the most musical member of the family I did feel a strong obligation to acquire some proficiency at the piano in view of my brother's sacrifice. There were of course several girls in school who could perform far better than I could yet for some reason I was appointed the school pianist and leader of the school dance band.

Having left school in 1942 and believing I would be sought after by a number of employers due to my success in the school certificate, I gave up both my part-time jobs. Unfortunately employers were not waiting to set me on for a number of reasons and even if they did due to the Government legislation the work would not have been of a permanent nature. Having given up my sources of income I found life more difficult and at the same time felt guilty through not contributing to the household.

From the age of sixteen I did service with the Fire Authority at night by sleeping at one of the local fire stations to act as a messenger boy in the event of fire resulting from bombing. For this service we were paid the sum of three shillings per night which meant at the end of the month there was something like one pound ten shillings in payment. During my period with the fire service together with two or three other lads we were taught to drive fire engines which stood me in good stead later in life.

Eventually through an old school friend I got news of temporary work in Lloyds Bank in Stony Stratford. The Manager gave me a test before setting me on which I could have passed when I was about twelve, completely ignoring the school certificate of which I was very proud. The work was difficult because I had not been trained in book-keeping. I and the other three staff regularly worked more than twelve hours every week-day and about seven hours on Saturday. There were no overtime rates. I was quite certain I was never going to get my job back. I must have been one of the worst bank clerks Lloyds ever had. It occurred to me to seek another job before joining the services where there may have been a better chance in the event of me surviving the war. Consequently I sought work with what was then the London Midland & Scottish Railway. Again after a pathetic examination still ignoring the school certificate I was given temporary work in the accounts department in Wolverton. The work was a total bore and we were obliged to work overtime every night until quarter to eight and Saturday we usually finished at mid-day. I had to stick it out for almost a year during which time I was registered and had a medical examination ready to be called up to the forces on my eighteenth birthday.

I was posted to Glasgow and arrived there on 1st June 1944. I found the city and the general hustle and bustle very frightening indeed but upon reaching the barracks became more settled and felt that I could respond to the physical and mental ability training I was to receive. Again I found army life in the main suited me. I was certainly able to perform in the mental tasks better than average. Physically I was able to hold my own dismantling and reassembling machine guns, understanding the use of arms and grenades, map reading and the other subjects which the army were teaching. All this was reasonably easy for me to assimilate. Despite that I had not really developed physically and along with half a dozen other men who were called up to Glasgow on the same day was graded as under-nourished and we were labelled as the milk babies. On parade in the morning each of us was given a pint of milk to consume accompanied by tumultuous cheers and ribald remarks from the rest of the men. Perhaps they didn't know that I thoroughly enjoyed the milk.

In September 1947 I was earmarked to take one months' rehabilitation leave where we went to live in a civilian situation got accustomed again to the ways of non-military life. I was sent to Coventry for this purpose where my eldest brother was a founder and for twenty years the Secretary of a CIU working men's club known as Coombe Social. This club permitted membership at the age of eighteen and my brother had enrolled me as a member when I first became a soldier so that I was able to use the club. My brother William demonstrated the way in which he kept the books of the club and I took the opportunity in the evenings to assist him to make some of the entries and balance the accounts. He suggested that I register with the CIU for their

Club Management Diploma which began about that time and the course ran through until the following May. This I did and as I still had several months to serve before demobilisation the Union posted the lessons to my army address. I often wondered if I was the only serving soldier who studied for the CMD.

Whilst on this rehabilitation exercise my Father died and I was granted five days compassionate leave to attend his funeral. At the end of this leave the day before I was to return to barracks I met for the first time, Gladys the girl I was to marry.

I finally went on demobilisation leave on 14th November 1947. The leave was for eight weeks and my conversion to a civilian began on 9th January 1948. I applied for my temporary job on the railway to be made available which it was and I commenced work there three weeks after demob leave started. In May 1948 I sat the CMD examination which then took place from ten o'clock in the morning with an hour break until five o'clock on a Sunday. There were no tutors and previous papers were not available. Consequently I had no idea what the examination would look like. I had however studied hard and failed the Law but I did, pass the accounts I dared not do otherwise. Having seen a Law paper for the first time I knew, at least I was fairly confident I would pass it the next time, which I did in 1949 with Honours.

After being a demobilised soldier I obtained my job as a railway clerk, but was unable to use the clubs which I had learnt so much about. This was due to the lack of spare money as my girlfriend and I were saving to get married and buy a house.

At that time the National Executive were having problems with the Management of the Bucks Branch, which comprised of twelve clubs. One of which was Wolverton Central where I was a member. Unbeknown to anyone except the secretary Len Allen who was also the chief reporter of the Wolverton Express, the Branch was to be closed down by the National Executive at the end of 1949. Therefore in October of that year he resigned and arrangements were made for an election of a new secretary in January 1950. One evening on my way home from seeing my girlfriend Gladys, I was stopped about eleven at night near the club by the Chairman Fred Atterbury and a group of his friends.

He had been deputised to ask whether I was prepared to be nominated to serve as the Branch Secretary of the Bucks Branch. The salary he said was twelve pounds per annum and there was a further seven pounds to cover the cost of the heat, light and use of a room in my house for the Branch office. The difficulty as I foresaw it was to get elected. I therefore decided on an election campaign among the twelve clubs and in November and December preparatory for the forthcoming election I made written appeals to each club to support my candidature. There were five candidates in all two of them well known club men, one other was well known in politics and one of these was expected to win. The election took place at Stony Stratford in January 1950 and much to the surprise of the other contestants I won by a small majority.

C. Bissell	8 votes
D. Dormer	10 votes
B. Stanton	8 votes
G. Burrows	3 votes
D. Bonner	nil votes

So the next official address of the Bucks Branch was 106 Jersey Road which was the house above and behind a Co-Operative Butchers shop where my mother and father had brought up twelve children. Gladys and I married in September 1950 and the address then moved to 89 Anson Road which was about fifty yards away.

The Branch Executive decided to invite the Club Union National Executive to hold its monthly meeting in the Bucks Branch in December of that year without realising that the National Executive had decided to close down the branch. In view of the replacement of the secretary the decision was put in abeyance until an assessment could be made of the new secretary's performance. On moving to Anson Road there was ample accommodation and we were able to allocate space for a branch office where stores could be accommodated and evening meetings could take place. In 1951 I sought election and succeeded in becoming a member of Wolverton Central Club Committee at the same time I wanted to make the branch an efficient unit. I enjoyed the book work particularly the figures. I enjoyed writing letters, I enjoyed meetings, I enjoyed visiting clubs quite often by bicycle up to ten miles each way, occasionally I would go by taxi.

Men twice, three times my age were beginning to consult me about club management and I did build up a huge reputation. I was already making plans to seek election to the National Executive Committee but I was interested in other things such as politics, trade Unions, football, cricket, gardening and generally enjoying life. The house Gladys and I bought had a bathroom and front and back gardens. A reasonable staff job at the railway gave me a pension to look forward to. But the office was like a prison and I knew I would not spend the rest of my life in a railway job.

Towards the end of 1951 I received a letter asking advice as to how to establish a Working Men's Club in Leighton Buzzard. This was a reasonable size town and it should have had a Working Men's Club many years previous. I wrote back and said if this person were to convene a general meeting of the public I would be happy to go to Leighton Buzzard and address the crowd and explain all that was necessary to be done.

Arrangements were made for a car hire firm to convey me on a dreadfully cold and bitter evening. In my mind I was excited by the prospect of speaking to a large crowd, demanding and thirsting for knowledge and information and I was the man to provide it. For a couple of weeks before the meeting I mulled over some of the things I would be saying. We arrived twenty minutes before the meeting was due to begin, and on a piece of waste land stood an old army Nissan hut which was the headquarters of the Labour party. My heart sank a little as I could not imagine the size of the crowd I had in mind all getting into this Nissan hut. Going inside, the hut was well lit and reasonably warm considering the inclement weather. A table had been arranged at one end and gathered around it were five people and two children. No more people arrived, not to be daunted I decided to give my best to this small group of five adults. The club was formed and known as Leighton Buzzard and District Labour Club. It soon developed and after some years established new premises and had been a classic example of Working Men's Clubs for some fifty years.

In 1952 I was regularly approached by officials of Stony Stratford Working Men's Club some of whom held rather high positions in the railway works. It seemed that the secretary who was a capable man was considering resigning. These gentlemen persuaded me to take on the position of Secretary of their beloved club. The club had moved into different premises in 1948 which had caused major financial difficulties. Originally it was on the Market Square in Stony Stratford but the building was sold to the council and became the head office of the Wolverton Urban District. The club purchased a house owned by a Colonel Hawkins of some local fame together with seven acres of land situated on the A5. Large areas of the land had been developed as ornamental gardens by the previous owner. Another large area was let as allotments to club members. In order to acquire this property and make some major changes to the structure it had been necessary to seek a loan of four thousand pounds from Lloyds Bank in Stony Stratford. The club struggled on, in March 1953 my son Thomas was born and later on that year after setting up the Club Union Midland Angling Championship I was persuaded by the gentlemen of high office in Wolverton works to seek election as the Secretary of their beloved club. There were no other candidates. The club had set a policy in order to meet their financial commitments of organising raffles at every opportunity. So having been appointed I insisted with the committee that no more raffles were to be held in the club or if they were held no one was to be asked to buy a ticket. If a member purchased a ticket he had to go to the table where they were sold. I had four different stewards in five weeks. Then I was told that together with the Trustees I was to attend one evening in the Managers office at Lloyds Bank to seek permission to carry on the club in view of the fact that the interest charges on the four thousand pounds had not been paid. I refused to attend as through my brief experience I knew that the club committee had been wrongly advised by the Manager regarding its finances.

Instead I contacted the Co-Operative bank in Northampton and then with the committee's support transferred the debt and the current account which had a healthy balance into one combined account reducing the debt to nearly half. Then with a system of careful planning within a very short number of years the debt vanished. When the news reached Lloyds Bank of this important loss of the business the Manager actually visited me at my house in Anson Road, pleading to keep the account. His plea fell on deaf ears, this was probably the saviour of Stony Stratford Club. Later in its history the club sold a parcel of its land for £350,000.

In 1954 Ernie Bexton who was Secretary of the Northants and Beds Branch and a member of the National Executive Committee called a meeting of branches in the Midlands at Coventry Working Men's Club in Cox Street on 13th March. There were delegates from Warwickshire, West Midlands, Leicester, Derby, Northants & Beds and the Bucks Branch which I represented.

The idea was to form a committee and organise an angling contest for teams and individuals in the Midlands area. I came away as its Secretary with the task of organising a Midlands Angling Championship for teams and individuals that year. This I did from my front room and it was staged on the Oxford canal most of which was rented to the Coventry Angling Association. Some six hundred anglers took part, to me it was a great challenge to organise this competition efficiently. It was highly successful and at the meeting held later in the year the committee was so delighted they unanimously agreed to donate me the sum of twelve pounds for my efforts. It was these twelve pounds I used to buy my first watch – I was twenty seven. The following year I continued, this time on the Grand Union Canal between Wolverton and Bletchley in North Bucks. Over six hundred anglers took part again and I was very pleased in the way the contest was carried off.

One year later in 1954 a vacancy occurred on the National Executive Committee of the CIU caused by the death of Ernie Bexon. At that time the Bucks Branch was joined with the Northants and Beds Branch to form one area to represent at National level. Bucks had twelve clubs and Northants & Beds had some eighty-two.

It had always been thought that as Northants and Beds had eighty clubs and the Bucks branch twelve it could never ever happen for anyone in the Bucks branch to win. Walter Thurston who had been secretary of the Bucks branch from 1902 until 1940 sought election about twenty times and always lost. I decided to canvas in a way similar to my previous efforts. Five candidates sought election one from Kettering, one from Bedford, one from Wellingborough and one from Northampton. I knew that by so doing the Northants and Beds branch was severely splitting its vote. If I could keep the Bucks branch which incidentally I didn't as two clubs voted against me and steal two or three clubs from each of the divisions I could win, that is what happened.

Dormer, Derek James,	Wolverton Central WM	- 51 votes
Osbourne, Reuben Joseph,	Irthlingborough Town Band	- 44 votes
Letts, Charles Arthur,	Kettering United Trades	- 41 votes
Walding, Edward Fred,	Northampton WM	- 37 votes
Tompkins, Frederick Charles,	Bedford Liberal	- 8 votes
Munton, Horace,	Kettering Rifle Band	- 3 votes

That was in November 1954 and I had a year to prove myself to Northants and Beds before they might decide to beat me at the next election.

The following year in 1955 I was due to seek election for the full two year term. This election I won by an overwhelming majority, the result was Dormer, Derek James ....176 and Davis, Kenneth John....14. So began my work at national level for the Working Men's Clubs on behalf of six million men and what became over four thousand Working Men's Clubs in Britain. It was a task I relished and despite my youth, still being in my twenties I was determined to improve things wherever possible.

Earlier in 1953 I had been appointed as a Union lecturer by the then Chairman of the Union's Education Committee, Sam Appleyard CMD, the Secretary of the Leeds Branch. Impressed with my essays on procedures at meetings and chairmanship, he became my mentor. He above all was delighted with my achievement in becoming elected to the National Executive Committee and I was immediately appointed to his committee, which controlled the Education Department of the Union.

The following year I was invited to give my first official lecture by the South Wales Branch one Saturday in Cardiff. The practise was for there to be two lecturers, one in the afternoon and the second one in the early evening after a break for tea. My co-lecturer on this occasion was the Union National President, Mr. Ted McEnery who was a brilliant orator and a formidable lecturer. After tea when I came to make my first attempt at giving a talk, I was extraordinarily nervous. I had prepared notes which I expected to last about an hour but found that I had completed all I had to say within thirty minutes. The audience was very kind to me indeed and I well remember one clubman saying to me after the event, I should learn to stand still when giving a talk to keep the audiences' attention. That kindly advice at that time stood me in good stead for the next fifty-six years during which time I must have delivered at least two thousand lectures.

About the same time that I was elected as a CIU Branch Secretary I also had a promotion in the accounts department of the British Rail. My work involved checking contracts for the supply of materials. At that time the supply of steel to various industries was rationed but the railways received thousands of tonnes in fact Wolverton works alone had an annual ration of four thousand tonnes of mild steel.

At that time the basic cost per ton of mild steel was £18.00. I found great interest in studying the steel contracts as well as those for many other commodities required for the construction of railway carriages and wagons. Often I would take the contracts home and study them in the evenings. There were a number of steel mills supplying the British Transport Commission from South Wales, The Midlands, Durham, the North East and Scotland generally as well as Yorkshire. I was somewhat mystified by the complexity of the system for determining the cost per tonne, and with the assistance of a lady named Sylvia Robinson who was a stenographer in the stores department, I began to write a procedure and the method of purchasing mild steel in its various forms. One thing which worried me particularly was that all the steel purchased by the British Transport Commission, and there were many thousands of tonnes annually, was required to be of machining quality. I began to wonder whether this was necessary and took it upon myself to talk to some of the four thousand workmen at Wolverton and to the technicians in the works as to the necessity of purchasing machine quality. It gradually emerged that only a very small quantity of this grade was required. As the steel industry which was then nationalised charged an extra one pound ten shillings per tonne a great deal of money was involved. I was also concerned by the way in which orders were given to have steel supplied in particular lengths. To do this the steel mills applied an additional charge for cutting different sections of steel into specific lengths. By talking to the workmen involved in the factory, I discovered that if the British Transport Commission purchased its steel in standard lengths we had the equipment and the know-how to cut the mild steel into the lengths required at a fraction of the cost being charged by the steel mills. I therefore, with the help of Sylvia Robinson produced a lengthy detailed suggestion, that the whole method of purchasing thousands of tonnes of steel annually for the British Transport Commission be changed. It did not need a change in the contract because the prices were laid down by the nationalised industry. When my suggestion was examined it was found to be faultless and the changes were brought about. I was instructed to travel to various other big centres Derby, Crewe and so on explaining the difference, and the British Transport Commission was better off to the tune of many thousands of pounds annually.

For this I was awarded the highest amount given for any suggestion from staff in 1954 the sum of fifty guineas. Later the British Transport Commission decided to give the best five suggestions received in that year a further prize, I was awarded the second highest prize and received a further seventy-five guineas.

Unfortunately this success attracted a great deal of publicity locally and I was earmarked for rapid promotion being sent to work at Headquarters in Euston for six months and also sent on a staff course at the college in Darlington to prepare me for a higher ranking position. At the same time I carried on with my Branch work helped by my wife Gladys in my absence, but the effect on the local population was extremely difficult and I suffered from a considerable amount of jealousy which I found impossible to live with. For example although my main club was the Wolverton Central, I had been a member of the Working Men's Social Club at Wolverton since 1950 and they were of course one of the thirteen clubs which were in the Bucks Branch. So severe was the jealousy of some local people that the management committee of Wolverton Social actually applied to the National Executive to transfer the club from the Bucks Branch to the neighbouring Northants and Beds Branch. As it happened the Northants and Beds Executive refused the request and the National Executive Committee rejected it absolutely. I often wonder how the members of that management committee could even face me after that, but they did when they were in trouble. 1958 had been quite an eventful year my mentor Sam Appleyard had died in the January and soon afterwards I gave the CIU fraternal greeting to the Annual Conference of the Workers Education Association at Harrogate, which was well received by the delegates. Later on that year on August 17th I organised the second of the Midland Angling Championships on the canal which stretched from Old Wolverton through to almost Bletchley. 1958 was also the year in which the Government passed a law to allow gaming machines to be operated in our clubs. At the end of 1957 the Government had produced a Bill entitled "The Children and Young Persons Bill" which was intended to outlaw the practise of families taking their children into the clubs for entertainment. The Union Executive opposed the Bill from its inception and were very active in parliament so that at its second reading in the chamber of the House of Commons the Bill was overwhelmingly defeated.

In 1959 I resigned from the railway and took up a job with one of the clubs' breweries as a travelling representative. This enabled me to allocate my working day and week between the brewery and the CIU much more conveniently. I developed the clubs brewery business by some seven hundred percent in my area during the five or six years I worked for them. The Board of the brewery then became difficult and instructed me one Saturday morning to give up the CIU, as they wanted my full-time attention. This I said I could not do and within the hour they dismissed me and instructed me to return my car to them on the Monday, which I did. When I returned home I resolved to work for myself and set up a company to carry out stocktaking in clubs by computer. This was in 1966, and by so doing I was able to carry out all the duties particularly lectures up and down the country without having to obtain permission from any other person. The Dormer stock reports became extremely well received and the company developed at a considerable pace.

I was of course interested in other aspects of education outside the Union and for several years attended as the fraternal delegate from the Union to the Workers Education Association Annual Conference. The Union, of course, had a Deed of Covenant to support this organisation.

Ruskin College, which had been set up in the early part of the century, was supported by trade unions, the Co-operative Society and the CIU for many years afterwards, I was a member of the college's council. Every year the Union gave a scholarship to a club member to study at Ruskin. Often these students went on to study at one of Oxford University's own colleges.

Manor House Hospital which had been set up by the trade unions also received considerable support from the CIU and had a close relationship with the Union's Convalescent Homes.

At the third meeting I ever attended of the National Executive held at Nantwich Convalescent Home in February 1955 a proposal was submitted by Sam Appleyard to change the name of the CIU to National Club and Institute Union. A lengthy debate ensued at the meeting the motion was eventually carried by one vote fourteen to thirteen. In those days the Union held delegate meetings every three months at various venues across Britain. There was not time to prepare this for the Blackpool Conference in April therefore the proposal to change the Union's name was to be considered at the quarterly Council Meeting in July of that year.

This Council meeting took place in the City of Leicester Working Men's Club and well over one thousand delegates were present. Quite a few were unable to gain access into the auditorium. That morning The Times carried in its leading article a fierce attack upon the National Executive Committee for this radical suggestion that the wording `Working Men's' be dropped from our title. There was huge opposition from across the country. Sitting on the stage listening to the attacks upon the National Executive which I had only recently joined was quite frightening. One of the most lasting impressions on me was the wonderful manner in which Ted McEnery the then President handled the meeting. It was, in my view the most remarkable demonstration of first-class chairmanship I had ever witnessed and I have never seen anything like it since. I then realised McEnery was an outstanding personality and endeavoured to learn as much as I possibly could from him. Later on these lessons were to stand me in good stead.

For many years the Union had been active in organising and sponsoring various games and recreational activities for its members, these contests were mainly indoors involving card games, billiards, snooker and so on. At the same time working people often found great pleasure in angling and for a number of years the Union had organised National Angling Contests which used to attract over one thousand individual anglers every year.

As the methods of angling varied somewhat across the country the Branches in the South of England decided to run an additional contest which they called the Southern Angling. This gave rise to the Midland Area Branches deciding to hold their own Midlands contest. These were in addition of course to the National.

I was beginning now to earn something of a reputation for myself as an organiser, certainly where angling was concerned. The Union appointed me to control the National Angling Championships and these were held on the Welland in Lincolnshire. The northern regional branches decided they wanted their own regional angling contest and I was asked to go to a meeting in Leeds and explain to them how to develop the organisation for such an activity. By the late Fifties I had become established as the Union's angling contest secretary.

At the same time my lectures were becoming more and more in demand across the whole of England and Wales and to some extent Scotland at Day or Evening Schools.

Every year the Union had for some time held residential courses, firstly at Ruskin College. This took the form of two separate weeks during the Easter vacation. Hundreds of applications were received and there was considerable competition to attend. Local Branch Executives selected from their members, the successful applications. Due to this huge demand for knowledge in the matters of club law, bookkeeping and administration, the Union was looking to extend its residential programme. During this period of the early Fifties Leicester College did apply for University status and the Club Union were among the sponsors to bring this about. As a consequence there was a connection between the University and the Union, which gave rise to the Union extending its residential courses by using Beaumont Hall in Leicester University for a week's course in the summer. This worked quite successfully for several years but I noticed that there were even more applications for residential courses in the summer at Leicester and I suggested that we had two weeks at Leicester and reduced Ruskin to one week as the accommodation at Ruskin was not so numerous as at Leicester. In this way we were able to accommodate more students. About that time Ruskin College acquired an additional building and together with Gladys, I attended the opening of this with the then Secretary of State for Education Mr. Anthony Crosland. However the site was too far from the original building for us to utilise it for our courses.

The thirst for knowledge seemed insatiable and in addition to Leicester and Ruskin we were able to obtain Easter holiday courses for Good Friday, Easter Saturday, Sunday and Monday at Durham University where we could accommodate some fifty students. Over and above these venues we then obtained the opportunity to hold weekly residential schools at Wentworth College in Yorkshire and for several years we utilised their facilities for two weeks in the summer time.

I was by then well known for delivering lectures on several different subjects and attended all of the schools. In most years, with these and evening schools, which I inaugurated, I was giving somewhere between fifty and sixty lectures every year.

In 1969 there were 3800 clubs with 3,250,000 individual members. In those days many clubs had their own lending library and reading room. In 1938 Wolverton Central had carried out extensions to the club which included a magnificent reading room and library. It was possible to read all the national daily papers, most of the national weekly and monthly magazines and something I was particularly interested in, the weekly Hansard. Once every three months an auction was held in the club for members to purchase these periodicals and newspapers. If you were successful you could take a daily paper at eleven o'clock at night for that day and the evening paper the following morning. Periodicals were taken when the next one arrived and I was successful several times in bidding for the copies of the weekly Hansard and I amassed dozens of these as a consequence. The lending library was open twice a week and it was common to see men hurrying to the club with two or three reading books under their arms and a couple of hours later emerging with books for their wives to read.

The interest in education provided by the Union and its clubs began to wane in the late eighties and early nineties and all of these residential courses were, one by one, abandoned and cancelled and the Union reverted to holding short weekend courses once or twice a year in Saltburn Convalescent Home.

Finding myself at the tender age of twenty-seven a member of the Club Union Executive, it was with some apprehension I set off to attend my first meetings. This was at the beginning of December 1954 and the meetings were to be held in Wakefield. In those days most of the Union Executive Committee meetings were held in the provinces, with one usually each year normally December in London. The Secretary of the Wakefield Branch was Ted McEnery CBE who doubled up as National President. It was often the custom then to meet in the Council Chambers and my first Committee meeting was held in the Mayors' Parlour in the City of Wakefield. The Mayor at the time being Alderman Alf Carr JP who as it happened was the representative of the Wakefield Branch on the National Executive Committee.

Needless to say I refrained from making any contribution at the meeting being somewhat overwhelmed, nervous and anxious to learn. As always the Local Authority entertained us to lunch in the hall and present were a few people not directly concerned with the National Executive Committee. Obviously these were comprised of Council representatives, Members of the Wakefield Branch Executive Committee and a well known newspaper crime reporter.

This man was John Hunt-Crowley a chain smoking whisky drinking Scottish newsman. By now he was working for Kemsley Newspapers one of the Tory Press Barons. Incidentally Hunt-Crowley had fought a parliamentary election as a Labour candidate and failed. Hunt-Crowley was famous later for his involvement in the Profumo affair having overheard a comment whilst commuting to his London office.

Profumo was the Member of Parliament for Kettering and a member of the Tory Government. He was disgraced through his relationship with a girl named Christine Keeler who was well-known among a certain wealthy section of the community. Hunt-Crowley had earlier, about 1951 found himself drinking in the Central Club which was part of the Union's Head Office building in Clerkenwell Road. The reason for his attraction was the fact that the Club was frequently visited by two well-known characters named Jack Spot and Joe Dime. Each of these had a number of followers and Hunt-Crowley was anxious to know more about their dubious activities.

During the course of his work he met and spent much time with the President of the Union Ted McEnery who was also partial to a little whisky. Although Hunt-Crowley was known by sight to most of the Executive and certain branches some like myself who were obliged to visit Head Office from time to time we were all nevertheless taken by surprise to find Hunt-Crowley in Wakefield. We stayed in a wonderful hotel known as the Stafford Arms, nobody was aware of the purpose of Hunt-Crowley's visit, it was not just for he and McEnery to get substantially inebriated.

During the next month or so all was revealed. Hunt-Crowley had changed from crime reporting to become Kemsley Circulation Manager. He had offered to use his skills to improve the circulation and profitability of the Club Journal. A contract was drawn up which as far as I know was not seen by any ordinary member of the Union Executive. Later on some of the clauses did become known to us and it transpired that Hunt-Crowley had plans to sell advertisements in an aggressive way to increase the profitability of the Journal. However it mattered not whether the Journal became viable financially because Hunt-Crowley was to receive fifty percent of the revenue from advertisements come what may.

There was of course a restriction on the amount of advertising, this was held at fifty percent of the total content. This did not worry Hunt-Crowley as he then began to pack the Journal with all manner of irrelevant rubbish, so there was no real limit to his adverts. Indeed one outspoken member of the Executive named Albert Linstead who was also Secretary of South Yorkshire asked when we might expect two or three pages of the Journal to be filled with information about breast feeding. I do believe this contract was changed at some point, not necessarily to the Unions advantage and it continued for three years after Hunt-Crowley's demise. I was particularly irritated when the Journal changed to colour printing and the front cover being in full colour was solely devoted to advertising. It was my belief, but difficult to prove that as we only got fifty percent of that revenue it almost certainly was produced and distributed with that page being a considerable loss to the Union. Needless to say I raised the issue countless times.

There was always a brick wall whenever questions of criticism regarding the Journal arose. I was determined even in those days that should I ever have the power and or influence that the Journal would be controlled by a Sub-Committee and therefore ultimately each month the Union Executive would oversee its production. I tried many times to bring the control within the Education Committee without success. Ultimately on becoming President in 1981 I was able to persuade the Executive to adopt this method.

Before departing from Wakefield on that bitterly cold December Sunday morning I was shocked that at seven o'clock many were drinking pints of draught bitter whilst waiting for their taxis. My second meeting of the National Executive was held in Newcastle upon Tyne, a town I had never ever previously visited and it seemed a long way to me. At that time the Union was obliged according to its constitution to hold a meeting known as the National Council four times a year, January, April, July and October. These were held in various parts of the country, occasionally in London. Generally there were five or six hundred delegates from Clubs and sometimes considerably more than that. They were almost always attended by the local Mayor and several members of Parliament. The January 1955 Union National Quarterly Council meeting was held in the City Hall in Newcastle. We had travelled to Newcastle a day earlier and whilst there the normal Executive meetings were held. The procedure was for the Convalescent Homes and Recreational and Educational Committees to meet on the evening that we travelled. The Finance had met the week before and the National Executive met the next morning. Then we reviewed the Finance report which was a written document. The other Committees reported verbally.

On the Friday afternoon we were taken on a tour of the Federation Brewery which was owned by Union clubs. In the evening the Executive was split into five or six groups and I remember travelling to the Throckley Union Jack Club. Having been warned by Sam Appleyard who was Education Chairman. Sam's words on that occasion stayed with me forever. He said to Bernard Holleworth from Chesterfield "you two young men remember that in the North East the beer is strong and the hospitality overwhelming" Bernard and I had been allocated a Rolls Royce from the Brewery to visit Throckley along the Tyne. Bearing the warning in mind we were not over late in returning. We drove along the Scotswood Road in this Rolls Royce stopping on the way for fish and chips, we ate in the back of the car. Reaching the County Hotel we sat like two goody goodies, reasonably well imbibed and certainly well fed and about midnight three or four men staggered through the foyer door carrying one person who was completely comatosed and taking him to bed. Next morning we asked Sam if he remembered being carried in!

On the Saturday afternoon we had this wonderful National Council meeting. I had been to these occasions previously as a delegate, but this time as a young man of twenty-seven, I was on the platform and introduced to the Council for the first time. I remember the problem of getting through that meeting without a cigarette as it was the first no smoking meeting I had ever been in. My next big occasion in kicking off this career was the second introduction from the platform at the Blackpool Conference. During that time the Annual Conference at Blackpool was often not as big as some of the regional National Councils owing to travel costs. But by this time the attendances were beginning to grow a little from the figure of between four hundred and six hundred in the early fifties. Attendances grew so that by the eighties the Union would receive possibly two thousand five hundred applications and normally about two thousand two hundred delegates would attend.

The reason I believe for my success initially in winning the vote for a seat on the National Executive was that I had by 1954 created something of a reputation for giving lectures mainly on chairmanship and procedure at meetings. I also had earned some credit for organising large scale Union angling contests. Even so this was no guarantee that when the bi-annual elections took place at the end of 1955 that I would get sufficient support. I therefore needed to impress the Northants and Beds Branch also the Bucks Branch Executive Committee and Council of my suitability to continue to represent them.

Earlier on in that year I made a serious mistake at a meeting of the Northants and Beds Council in February at Finedon Gladstone Club. About one hundred delegates attended and they had come as much as anything to hear the General Secretary Frank Castle, and myself their newly elected National Executive man. Among other things I stated that I did not believe women should be allowed in a Working Men's Club bar. I should explain that the Bucks Branch certainly held this view but in Northamptonshire they were of the opinion mostly that women ought to be welcomed in the bar. I was given the bird in no uncertain terms and I have to confess it did not take long for me to change my view.

When the elections were near the Northants & Beds Branch Executive Committee decided that my performance had not been completely disastrous and they were willing to give me a chance and not oppose me so I should be safely elected for the following two years. In the event I was opposed by a candidate from my own Branch he was from Bletchley Working Men's Club, which was the club visited every night on the way home from Fleet Street by a gentleman named John Hunt-Crowley who had learned to suspect me now. Although I had no proof it was pretty clear at that time he was instrumental in opposing my candidature. I won the election with three clubs voting against me all from among the twelve members of the Bucks Branch. Apart from Bletchley the other two were Stantonbury Social and Wolverton Social. When the results were announced and we met in January 1956 in Doncaster Trades and Labour Club, I well remember Billy Ollerton who was later awarded the Queens Jubilee Medal he represented the Manchester Branch and was Secretary of Acre Gate Labour Club, Preston saying to me that my win was the best on the coupon.

Early Work With The National Executive – Centenary Celebrations

The next few years were extremely busy, my son, Thomas had been born in 1953 and was now beginning to grow up and Gladys who I had by necessity left many hours days and nights alone with Tommy felt that they wished to be with me more often. Consequently wherever possible especially at seaside towns I was accompanied by them on most trips. At the same time because of my work on the railway, I was under pressure from the railway authorities and began to look for other employment.

Firstly an opportunity arose in the Head Office of the Union for a new Assistant General Secretary as Tommy Nichol the long serving former holder of this office had retired. The position was to be filled by the National Executive at its monthly meeting in the Variety Artists Club Birmingham. Being a member of the Executive of course, I did not take part in the appointment and remained outside the room with the other principle candidate John Holmes. We waited together outside the meeting and when called in were informed that the Executive had appointed John to the post. Afterwards we had a drink together and I said to John that I would support him when the time came for the General Secretary-ship and he very kindly guaranteed to support me should I seek the President's office. We worked together for a number of years. However I was still looking for alternative employment.

This came in 1956 when I was appointed the sales representative of Northants & Leicester Clubs Brewery which was later changed to the Midlands Clubs Brewery. I was very happy doing this work, mobile and able to continue Club Union, Branch and Brewery work for the benefit of all three. I was able to increase the sales of club brewery beer over a two year period by seven fold.

In 1960 my daughter Linda was born and I did feel that I had a very happy family. My mother lived nearby with my brother Jack, Gladys's mother and father lived not far away with her brother David.

I was beginning to feel reasonably successful and was anxious to give Gladys and the children a good life. One thing I wished to do was to find a more modern house for Gladys to bring up the children and for her to enjoy her surroundings. We spent some time searching possible alternative areas in which to live providing they were convenient for my brewery work and eventually we settled in Higham Ferrers, Northamptonshire. The Union benefitted from this move as well as myself and the Brewery. In 1966 Charlie Hobbs CMD who had been Secretary of the Northants and Beds Branch since 1954 died suddenly. The Branch whose Secretary was a part-time job and I knew that if I did not seek election whoever did would, if he had a mind to, defeat me as the National Executive representative. The only way out of this dilemma was for me to seek election as the Secretary of the Branch. The week before the election was due to take place the Brewery board gave me one hour to change my mind or sack me.

I felt I had no option and stood for Secretary against four other candidates the following Saturday. There were one hundred and seven delegates and I got eighty-six votes. The meeting was at Bedford North End Club and I well remember Gladys' anxious face waiting on the doorstep for me with Linda because she did not know whether I had a job or not. She was quite relieved.

1957 was a very busy year and much was happening indeed there was a revaluation of business properties brought about by the Miscellaneous Provisions Act. In my role as Secretary of the Bucks Branch I was continually arguing with the Inland Revenue Valuation Officer at Aylesbury. He had suggested that clubs should call upon their members to pay an economic subscription to enable them to pay rates on the increased assessment. However, I did appeal on behalf of all members clubs in the Bucks area and was successful in every case in obtaining a considerable reduction in the rating valuation of the Working Men's Clubs. The argument was, of course, that Valuation Officers tended to regard clubs as a business. I had to pursue the point that a club could not trade or carry on a business for profit and therefore the business rates as applied to public houses could never apply to member's social clubs. Most valuations of clubs were done on a comparison basis with one another in any locality. Whilst all this was going on the Union was very active in making appeals against assessments for our Convalescent Homes, on the same basis.

In 1958 the Union began to think about the possibility of celebrating its centenary which would fall on the 14th June 1962. Various comments were made about the way in which this milestone should be celebrated. In order to be positive, I moved a motion at the meeting of the Executive in Morecombe that year to form a centenary committee. This received a majority of votes from the Executive and they then set about electing a sub-committee. It consisted of the President and five members of the National Executive Committee including myself.

The centenary committee as it was called began to have regular meetings. It was decided that the major celebration would take the form of building a new Head Quarters somewhere in London. The President's idea was that the building should in addition to providing office space would include a hotel, and a model Working Men's Club. When these proposals were put to the National Executive, there was opposition. Virtually no member of the Executive considered that the project was feasible. The criticism of the committee was severe and some of the cynics began to refer to the centenary committee as the cemetery committee. I assumed that they felt the project we had in mind would destroy the Union.

The next job was to find a suitable site, not too far from a railway terminus and John Laing who were renowned for building throughout the country, Coventry Cathedral being one of their prize developments were appointed to obtain a suitable area for us to build what we had planned. The committee were taken around to see various possibilities throughout London. We probably saw some fifteen or twenty sites, all of which were rejected for one reason or another. We then widened the instruction to Laings saying that the site need not necessarily be close to a railway terminus. Eventually after about one year of searching, we decided on Highbury Corner, Islington, and proceeded to secure the area and appointed architects.

Eventually the new offices were completed providing first-class adequate office space, a wonderful boardroom for the National Executive and because of the way in which the proposals for changes were made the building also included the model club`s concert hall and balcony.

During the many meetings and debates we had to bring about the construction of the premises, I proposed that it included an underground car park. No one on the committee agreed with my view that one day some people would go to work by car and travel to London for other reasons by motor car rather than by train. So my proposal to have an underground car park was never agreed by the centenary committee. However when the final plans as drawn up by the architects were submitted to London County Council, they were rejected unless the proposal included an underground car park Therefore this was brought about and provision was made for some sixteen cars to be parked under the building.

Gradually under severe pressure even McEnery began to buckle and first the printing works went and then the hotel, then the club. It should be noted that the motion to remove this club somehow failed to remove the concert hall which was retained in splendid isolation, a real white elephant. But the building went ahead on the site which Laings had found us which at the time we inspected it housed a fairground with dodgem rides, coconut shies and the rest.

The cost included the purchase of land and additional land on which stood some factories and other parcels of land plus all professional fees and the actual construction a total bill was presented of one hundred and forty-six thousand pounds. As we had sold Clerkenwell Road for eighty thousand pounds the sixty-sixty thousand pounds we had to spend did not appear to us to be irresponsible. As the building neared completion, copies of the plans were handed to the heads of department to suggest an allocation of space for the personnel and equipment. The staff's ideas of office requirements shocked me beyond belief the visions of grandeur some must of had as to the size of their personal office was breathtaking. The Centenary Committee did not seem to understand this. I therefore took the plans home and re-designed the whole of the interior in such a way that the third floor was left vacant. When I explained and demonstrated my plans to the Centenary Committee I argued that the building was constructed to allow for expansion of the Union which at the time was developing rapidly. If we used all the space now what would happen in ten years time? My theory was accepted and I suggested that we let the top floor on a seven year lease from time to time until we required if for ourselves. The Union successfully let the third floor at an annual rent of two thousand five hundred pounds plus heating and cleaning costs. The actual area of the floor was around three thousand two hundred and sixty-five square feet. We did manage to let the top floor and John Holmes then Assistant General Secretary was given one thousand pounds for doing so.

It was also decided that a book should be published to coincide with the centenary entitled "Our 100 years" and George Tremlett from Coventry was appointed the author. The committee was also anxious that the building would be opened officially exactly one hundred years to the day the Union was created. Therefore the opening ceremony would be held on the 14th June 1962.

Ted McEnery was determined that the opening ceremony would be performed by the 6th Earl of Rosebury as his grandfather the 4th Earl had been instrumental in creating the Union with the Reverend Solly and others and had been its President before he transferred to 10 Downing Street to be the Prime Minister. However the 6th Earl was not particularly interested in carrying out this ceremony so he was informed, in that case we would ask his son and heir Lord Primrose Rosebury to act in his stead. On hearing of this decision the 6th Earl decided that he would after all perform the opening ceremony.

When the day came we had made preparations for the opening to be conducted in a very formal manner with champagne and two great speeches, one by McEnery and one by the Earl himself. We had commissioned for a silver salver to be produced and suitably engraved. The words on the silver salver read,

Presented to
THE RT HON THE EARL OF ROSEBERY.K.T.D.S.O.M.C.
on his opening
Club Union House London
The New Headquarters of the
Working Men's Club & Institute Union
Commemorating the Union's Centenary
14th June 1962

The Earl at the end of his speech, opening the building, held the silver salver aloft and declared that it would remain in his family forever. Some years later Gladys purchased this silver salver at Mentmore House and it is currently in my family's possession.

Early Work In Parliament

There was a further item of legislation known as the Betting and Gaming Act 1960 which was designed to permit the lawful use of gaming machines, commonly known as fruit machines in private members clubs.

At a meeting held at Eastbourne on Saturday 3rd December 1960 the National Executive of the Union passed the following motion:- "The Union Executive holds the view that automatic gaming machines are undesirable things to be installed in Union

Clubs quite apart from any question of their legality, and they have decided that they will not assist or undertake to finance the defence of any Club which is prosecuted in connection with the use of such machines. The Executive do not sponsor or recommend them to Union Clubs". In September 1966 the Union had expressed its serious objection to any form of casino type gaming relating to roulette and in particular gaming machines. At the same time the Union's insurers were instructed not to cover any gaming machines through the Union's insurance agency. There was utter rejection of gaming by the Union Executive.

The Union Executive instructed Branch Secretaries to pursue its opinion as regards the dangers of gaming machines being introduced into our clubs.

After a few months I was informed by the oldest club in Northamptonshire, Northampton Working Men's, situated then in St. Giles Street, they had introduced two of these machines for their members.

When I spoke to the Secretary Mr. Dan Woodward, he explained to me that in the first week the club had taken the magnificent sum of forty pounds from the two machines. This was a large amount and he and his committee held the view that they could not possibly reject this form of income if it were to regularly reach this kind of figure. When it became fairly well-known in the vicinity, almost overnight, every club in Northamptonshire, Bedfordshire, Buckinghamshire and indeed the rest of the country were installing gaming machines. One or two clubs, particularly in the north held out against them for a few more years, but they had come to stay.

During this part of the Union's history there was considerable support and loyalty displayed by clubs, Branches and individual members towards the organisation. By the end of 1962 I had thirteen years' experience as an officer of the Union including some nine years on the National Executive.

I was extremely dedicated and enthusiastic and was well aware of the need for the Union to be financially sound if it were to continue to carry out its objective of protecting the movement from any detractors.

At the November meeting of the Executive in 1962 I raised the question of copyright fees for the Union model rules. For many years the Union had produced model rules for clubs registered under either the Industrial & Provident Societies or the Friendly Society Acts, as in certain aspects the rules were different to cover the specific requirements of the Acts. Much work and investigation went into the production of these model rules and from time to time clubs updated their rules as was necessary by law changes or for other reasons. The Union always checked the amendment, after which through the Union Head Office the amendments were confirmed with the Registrar. At that point orders were placed for printing.

I had noticed that some clubs preferred to have their model rules when agreed with the Registrar to be printed privately. I did not object to this but felt that as the model rules were copyright, then clubs should pay a copyright fee if their printing was done other than through the Union's agent. I therefore raised this matter at the meeting in November. The Executive agreed with my opinion and it was resolved that in future when clubs made their statistical return to Head Office that they were to include two copies of their latest model rules. This was to enable Head Office staff to determine whether or not a copyright fee should be charged to the club.

1963 was a busy year for me in many ways. The Union continued its fight in Parliament to ensure that tombola could be played lawfully in our clubs and that in certain circumstances club funds could be used to provide a snowball. This was a special prize which was added to each week if it was not won. In order to win the snowball the player had to achieve a full house in the tombola under a certain number of calls.

The Union also opposed a Bill by the London County Council to allow for registration and inspection by police in Union clubs. In addition we pressed the Government to insist that brewers were compelled to display upon their products either on beer bottle labels or hand pumps for draught beer the actual original gravity. The reason for this pressure by the Union was that Excise Duty was levied according to the OG of the commodity. The alcoholic strength of a beer was not necessarily related to the original gravity and therefore does not indicate clearly enough the proportion of

Tax which a person is paying when purchasing the commodity.

In the same year the National Executive were concerned as to the management of its Monmouthshire Branch and the Union Vice President, Arthur Bates, together with Albert Linstead, the Secretary of South Yorkshire and myself were deputed to carry out an investigation into the management affairs of that office. I felt very much the junior in this situation and was over-awed by Albert Linstead, who could be a bully, but his knowledge of finance did impress me. This was, notwithstanding the fact that the Secretary of the Monmouthshire Branch at the time was a qualified Chartered Accountant.

Crewe Oddfellows club submitted a motion for the Union Council Meeting to set up a legal department at Head Office staffed by a qualified lawyer and assistant. This was defeated and rejected by the National Executive. Interestingly enough in 1981 when I became Union President I, without reference to the Executive appointed a qualified lawyer and gave him two staff to work with.

That same year the Union, in connection with Manor House Hospital, encouraged all clubs to become patrons of the Hospital at a subscription of two pounds two shillings per year. I together with three other colleagues from the Executive was invited to represent the Union at Her Majesty's Garden Party in July, this was my second visit.

I was elected as the National Union Vice President at a bi-election which was occasioned by the death of Ted McEnery CBE in 1969. I was a candidate for President to take his place but was defeated quite heavily by the then Vice President Arthur Bates who had served ten years in that post and who subsequently served a further eleven years as President. After my defeat I resolved to seek election as Vice President and was successful.

This achievement fulfilled a promise I had made in March 1956. The Executive met at the Birmingham Variety Artists Club for its monthly meeting. Four members of the Executive were absent that day. One of the principal subjects on the agenda was to appoint a new assistant General Secretary due to the retirement of Tom Nicol. I was a candidate and therefore not present during the discussion and voting and John Holmes was also an applicant having been the Unions Legal Assistant for about two years. John won fourteen- thirteen, myself and the other four absentees of course not voting. Having a drink afterwards in the bar together, I congratulated John promising every support and guaranteed that he would be General Secretary one day and I would be President. John was very disappointed when I failed at the first attempt and he being removed from office virtually when I succeeded on the second occasion. On reflection I felt certain that the Executive had made the right decision in preferring him to me. When he became General Secretary I was delighted.

John worked closely and amicably with Ted McEnery and the two were somewhat notorious for their drinking bouts. After McEnery's demise John found considerable difficulty in working with Arthur Bates and for that matter so did I. John's drinking got worse and he became almost entirely dependent on alcohol. But he could still write brilliant reports and he had the ability to unravel complex problems. He was always supported by a secretary, a girl named Anne.

During the last twelve months of his eight years of the high position he held, he took his work each morning to a hotel to avoid contact with staff and telephone calls and there his secretary Anne recorded his correspondence, and attended to the transcription and despatch in the afternoon sessions. He was also an accomplished speaker and gave hundreds of lectures.

Quite rapidly his reputation for drinking grew beyond acceptable levels. The Union Executive was deeply concerned and so was I. In 1973 we were expecting a huge voice of resentment and a call for his resignation from the delegates at Blackpool. I was deputed to arrange to see him and his secretary Anne and seek his resignation. He agreed to meet me with Anne and I fixed a room in the Hind Hotel at Wellingborough. I met them off the train and talked most of the day. We finally reached a settlement and only required an exact choice of words. I put John and Anne back on the train in the early evening and set off for Blackpool. At the EC meeting the next morning I reported to the Executive and worked most of that day and early on the Saturday morning to agree on the telephone the exact wording of the telegram he would send to the President to be read to the Conference.

Everybody was mightily relieved some like myself were also very saddened. Anne a very popular lady also resigned on Monday. At that time the Assistant General Secretary was Frank Morris. He was one of the applicants for the vacancy which had been created in the late sixties for the post of Assistant General Secretary which he failed to secure. Later when another post, that of the Legal Assistant had been unoccupied for some time the Union offered the position to Frank Morris.

After a short time the Assistant General Secretary Leslie Tibbs resigned and Morris got the job. John Holmes did not enjoy working with him and when John was virtually forced to resign Frank Morris won the election. I worked with him as well as possible but was always unsure of his loyalty to me as Vice President and indeed to the Union itself. But he was capable, he would write first class reports although he had a reputation for stretching the truth. Indeed he was certainly criticised for his arrogance and ignorance even in an Official Royal Commission Report into the Gaming Laws of Britain. When he retired in 1982 he was bitterly disappointed with the Testimonial Fund set up for him and accused me of failing to fulfil a promise regarding the extent of the Unions' contribution and we have never spoken again.

Throughout the 60's the Union was active in every way and was still growing there being 3800 clubs in membership by 1968.

For many years it had been the practise for the Union to seek an audience with the Chancellor of the Exchequer and normally this was granted. The President and General Secretary were allowed to make a plea for a reduction in beer duty. This never happened but the Union often felt that if the increase set out in the budget was restricted to an additional one penny per pint it could be regarded as a victory. It was more difficult when the Chancellor on occasions added two pence on a pint because we could only then regard that as a defeat.

1966 had been an eventful year for me, in January of the year I was elected as Chairman of the Union's Education Committee. I was also elected together with the President, Bill Ollerton and Norman Sharpe to form an advisory committee of the Union. The purpose of which was to assist and check correspondence particularly from the General Secretary to important areas of the Government or the Union generally. In March of the same year I was elected to the Executive Council of Ruskin College, Oxford. During the summer I was very active in promoting a new club in Towcester in conjunction with Bill Stephenson, who had been transferred in his work from Durham to this area where there was no club. I was instrumental in obtaining the finance from Courage Brewery to build the club. At an earlier meeting of the Union's Executive, I requested that the club be admitted to membership of the Union even before the building was complete. The Union Executive rejected my suggestion.

Advanced Work In Parliament

During the late seventies and eighties quite a number of examples of racial discrimination were alleged to have been taking place in some of our clubs. One particularly flagrant case occurred at the Barras Green Social Club in Coventry. This was like many others in that City extremely prosperous and very well managed, the Secretary being a man named Vic Terry. Together with Arthur Bates the President, Frank Morris the General Secretary, I was deputed to attend on the Club Committee to discuss the allegation that the Club apparently refused admission to a coloured member of a musical group which had been contracted to perform there. The Entertainers Trade Union were involved and the Union Executive viewed the issue with considerable concern. Arriving at the Club the three of us, the top three Officials of the Union were properly received, welcomed and offered hospitality. We were led to the Committee room where management, which comprised of about sixteen or eighteen members sat around a long oval table and we three were at one end. I was of course the junior of the three. As the meeting developed I became more and more shocked at the attitude of the Committee and the apparent support offered to them by my two colleagues. I was, I felt in a minority of one to twenty odd, but still feel ashamed that I did not have the moral courage to object. My respect for them such as it was, finally disappeared, as did the club a year or so later through the action of strong Trade Union picketing. The club was eventually taken over by a coloured group who I understand did not admit white people.

At that time the Union Annual Conference had grown, the

attendances reached between two thousand and two thousand five hundred delegates. The morning session was almost wholly occupied by speeches from invited guests, for example in 1967 the guests at the Blackpool Conference included the Mayor & Mayoress, both members of Parliament, fraternal delegates from the Clubs Breweries Association, Royal British Legion, Manor House Hospital, Workers Education Association, Dr. Horace King Speaker of the House of Commons and the General Manager of the British Law Insurance. The main speech during the morning session was the Presidential Address given by Mr. Ted McEnery. Most of these well-known speakers captivated the audience and set the mood for the afternoon session which was devoted to the business of the Union and consideration of its annual report.

Throughout this period among other activities the London University Department of Education had an arrangement to bring their overseas students to visit Head Office where they were given a talk by the General Secretary to explain how Working Men's Clubs fitted into the social life of the community of Britain. This department of London University also visited for a few days each year with their students Knuston Hall in Northamptonshire and while they were there I had the privilege of entertaining them and gave tours round the local clubs of Rushden and Higham Ferrers. Also on two occasions they visited my home in Higham Ferrers for a summers evening.

Race relations had been an issue in the Union for some time. When John Holmes first became General Secretary a serious case arose in Preston at the Dockers Club and we were sent to defend it. The defence argument being that the club in refusing to admit a coloured associate had not committed an offence because, and we proved this, an associate member of the CIU is not in that capacity a member of the public. Pretty thin grounds really. At the same time another case arose in East Ham where the Conservative club had a problem with a prospective coloured candidate. One day sitting in the Committee room with John Holmes and one or two other Senior Executive Committee members John put to us an application from the Association of Conservative clubs, through their then General Secretary to support their litigation in East Ham and we agreed to underwrite their costs in defending themselves to the tune of twenty-five thousand pounds. Their case did not go to Court. The Union of course has no particular affiliation nor does it officially support any party.

Among my list of ambitions was the creation of some form of Parliamentary representation. I remember in the fifties when I was first serving on the Union Executive it was necessary to spend quite a number of evenings in London. On occasions either in little groups or alone, I would wander to the House of Commons. The security was practically non- existent and it was possible to wander anywhere you wished by just exercising a little common sense. Frequently I would meet with other colleagues of the Union Executive and we would stand around in the bars enjoying a drink. I well remember on one of those occasions being taken by a Labour MP into the Gallery. Speaking at the dispatch box on that evening was Miss Pike who was either the Secretary of State for Education or at least a Minister. I often later thought that much of that time we spent was wasted, and determined if given half an opportunity to organise real representation. Therefore, after Don McMahon succeeded in having my list accepted, I spoke to Jack Johnson, who was by now General Secretary and knew quite a number of Labour MP's from the North East, to organise a little get together to advice on the question of creating something in Westminster. Jack fixed a lunch in a cafe in Upper Street and present were Lord Peart a former Government Minister, Lord Brooks for many years election agent to James Callaghan, Gordon Bagier MP for Sunderland, John McWilliams still an MP twenty years later for Blaydon, Jack Johnson, Colin Hughes and myself. It was a very fruitful meeting and we were advised to circulate a letter to all MP's. Gordon Bagier was to find a room in the House and a date to call an inaugural meeting to form an all party group. Before we could write the letter Mrs. Thatcher called an election for May, this had the effect of suspending our operations through the summer. By the time things were organised properly the date set for this historic meeting was December 14th 1983.

I was more nervous than usual and had spent some time in preparing a speech designed to persuade the Members of Parliament to create this force. Almost to the last minute Carol Goddard who worked as my Secretary for more than twenty years and Colin Hughes Chairman of Finance and Secretary of South Wales helped me to dot the I's and cross the T's. The moment came. We were met by Gordon Bagier in the Central Lobby and led to a committee room. Well before the published time to begin it was quite obvious the room was not large enough. Fevered re-organisation took place and we were then led to a large Committee room on the third floor. I had previously checked that it was in order to take with us a stenographer to record the proceedings. Because of the dreadful reputation we were enduring on the race issues, I selected Charmaine to accompany me as official note-taker. Charmaine of West Indian origin worked for the Club Union about thirty years. Jack Johnson refused this request for various reasons. When Gordon Bagier called the meeting to order one MP objected to we strangers being present in the room and we were promptly removed. After some five or ten minutes waiting in the corridor we were invited back and it was announced that the group had been incorporated and permission was given to me to address this newly formed organisation. Carol was invited to take notes at the official table. I was then introduced to make my speech. I protested that my prepared speech was designed to persuade the MP's to do what they had already done therefore it was superfluous.

At that point there was a chorus all demanding that I make the speech anyway. That was one of the kindest reactions I have ever experienced. I felt that these very important people had not lost anything by their elevated positions. I had a strong feeling they all, be it man or woman wanted to help me get through what may have been an ordeal and this is what I said,

Press Release 15th December 1983

At the instigation of the Working Men's Club and Institute Union, an all-party Parliamentary Sub-Committee of members of both Houses of Parliament has been formed in the interests of non-profit making members' social clubs. Other club organisations including the Association of Conservative Clubs, Royal British Legion, National Union of Liberal Clubs and the National Union of Labour Clubs, have indicated their willingness to be involved. Liaison with the Committee will be through the General Secretary of the Working Men's Club and Institute Union.

The meeting to officially form the committee was held last evening in the House of Commons, when 56 members signified membership and appointed the following officers:-

Joint office of Chairman - (G.A.T. Bagier M.P.
(G.B. Porter M.P.
Joint office of Vice-Chairman - (M.C. Welsh M.P.
(to be appointed)

Secretary – Lord Brooks of Tremorfa.

Apologies for absence were received from a number of members unable to attend owing to various commitments, each signifying their willingness to be included in the Committee.

Mr. D. J. Dormer, C.M.D., President of the Working Men's Club and Institute Union Ltd. Addressed the meeting in the following terms:-

J.JOHNSON
General Secretary.

My Lords, ladies, gentlemen,

Thank you for your time which I know is a scarce commodity among people charged with momentous responsibilities. The purpose of this meeting cannot be regarded as of paramount importance when viewed in the context of the numerous problems in international affairs, the economic situation with its attendant unemployment, the Nation's health and so on. Yet it is vitally important in the minds and everyday lives of millions of ordinary folk and their families.

There are some thirty thousand non profit making Members Clubs in Britain, many of which are grouped into associations formed for their protection. The largest of these, possibly the best known and certainly the oldest is the Working Men's Club and Institute Union, which has some four thousand clubs, with about six million members, male and female. As its President, I am delegated to speak on their behalf in this matter. My credentials do not permit me to act directly for the Association of Conservative Clubs which has some 1,400 member clubs, or the Royal British Legion with about a thousand clubs, but I feel that what I have to say will probably also apply to them. In addition there exist a number of smaller organisations and many clubs

which are not affiliated in any way. I have not been appointed to speak for them, but would point out that one of the Union's objectives is to protect any club, irrespective of whether it is in membership or not, provided that it fulfils the basic requirement of being democratically controlled and non-profit making.
It would be wrong of me to weary you with the long history of the Club and Institute Union or of the detailed problems which concern the Club movement at the present time, but I feel obliged to briefly outline both these subjects.

The Club and Institute Union, was the "brain child" of a Methodist Minister who, about the middle of the 19th Century, gained sympathetic support and financial assistance from the highest in the land. The principles and ideals laid down when it was weaned have not changed. It is we believe the greatest success story on the social scene in this country during these 125 years. It is neutral in matters of party politics, religion and has no ethnic prejudice, contrary to some opinion. It is obsessed with its democratic constitution. It is equally determined that everything done in its name is well within the law: its very existence creates law and order and where the law stops short, a strict code of self discipline is rigidly applied by the Union through to individual members. This system operates between the individual member and the club, based on the rules of natural justice, and there is an appeal procedure. Similarly when a charge is made by the Union against the club itself for example "bringing the Union into disrepute", the same principles apply. Any appeals being referred to arbitrators.

In the case of the Union they are:

Lord Gormley	Former President N.U.M.
Mr. Alan Davis of Ind. Coope.	Leader of the Employers Side of the L.N.R. Establishment Wages Council.
Sir William Richardson	Former Chief Executive – Co-op Press
Mr. Gordon Waterman	Gen.Sec. Association of Conservative Clubs

Mr. David Care	Gen.Sec. Manor House Hospital
Mr. John Hughes	Principal – Ruskin College Oxford.

Non profit making Members Private clubs are in effect an extension of people's homes – particularly working people. It is the place to which they may resort for purposes generally defined in the objects of the club as providing facilities for rational recreation, mental and moral improvement and social intercourse. In some cases there are additional objectives such as the support of a political party, a particular sport or a group of ex-servicemen and so on. In general, it is difficult to imagine what kind of social life there would be for ordinary working people were it not for member's clubs scattered throughout every city, town and village. Few would dispute the value to the Nation of these clubs which ask little help, if any, are self financing and provide an outlet for people who perhaps otherwise would never have an opportunity to display their talents in leadership, financial acumen, organisational ability or their willingness to serve their fellow men, many begin their political careers in this way. Occasionally one may read of some misdemeanours such as drinking after time or making a bet on a horse, which are regarded by some as the worst possible sins known to mankind. Rarely does one read of the vast contributions to charitable causes made by member's clubs or of the wonderful work in providing convalescent treatment every year for thousands of men and women. Nor is much reported of the work performed in the field of education and training.

During the last three years we have provided, in the C.I. U. training courses on a daily, evening, weekend, weekly or six monthly correspondence scheme, for nearly twenty thousand men and women. Each year the Club Union sponsors and organises over two thousand separate games championships on a local, county, regional and national basis. How many people realise that among the great names in snooker and darts, who now give so much pleasure through T.V., the majority have been nurtured through the C.I.U. The same may be said of many famous names in the entertainment world.

All good things, it is said, must come to an end. It appears to many of us concerned with the establishment, management and development of member's clubs today, that a "sinister force" has set about the task of proving this maxim. The harassment which is now being suffered virtually nationwide from police authorities and to a lesser but still dangerous degree by local authorities, Customs and Excise and Inland Revenue, is causing fear and confusion. In recent years there have been several Acts of Parliament which, on face value, appear to offer wider freedom to members clubs, have in fact planted the seed of destruction. Regulations have been made under existing Acts of Parliament which cause enormous difficulties, so much so that the resource of volunteer management is dwindling fast and there is reluctance to grapple with these almost incomprehensible laws, coupled with pressure exerted by various public authorities. It seems to us that much of this has been engineered deliberately to cause bewilderment and whereas it may be difficult to amend legislation, our objective is to prevent any further laws and regulations of this type making inroads into our security and restricting the freedom of the individual. I must make it clear we blame no-one but ourselves. We now realise that instead of taking these blows we ought to have organised resistance in Parliament long ago, by drawing attention to our case loud and clear. The only excuse we have to offer is that we are not by nature publicity seekers, and have tended to keep our difficulties to ourselves. Members of Parliament with the enormous pressures and problems facing them have no doubt allowed these Bills to become law possibly without realising the devastating effect they are having.

We do not expect to be isolated from the economic difficulties which have faced everybody and every organisation in recent years. We can always cope with this situation as we have done in the past. We cannot cope with the threats contained in circulars issued by Police Authorities (we have many examples) or with Acts of Parliament, for example the "Licensing (Occasional Provisions) Act, 1983, which can be interpreted in such a way as to permit police right of entry into private member clubs. That is certainly the understanding of the police when the unsuspecting club implements some of its clauses and that is why police authorities all over the country are recommending adoption of these clauses. In some cases (and we have evidence), the police are threatening to oppose renewals of Registration Certificates unless these clauses are adopted, giving them right of entry. There are other ramifications concerning the Revenue and the gaming laws.

Many clubs are registered with the Registrar of Friendly Societies and in some cases under the Company's Act. So far as the Union is concerned, it is a pre-requisite that a club must so register. We have a long tradition of working closely with the Registrar to safeguard the interests of our Members under Statute and to ensure that properly elected officers fulfil their obligations and ensure accountability. Even in this quarter there is no escape from official interference. Notwithstanding the fact that our model rules are framed exactly in accordance with law, this high ranking Civil Servant is presently insisting on a change simply because in his opinion it would be an improvement. Whereas we have no desire to have an altercation with such an authority, we are unable to accept that he knows best. We feel that we must be permitted to make our own decisions so long as we conform to the Law.

Perhaps the most pernicious threat to the very existence of non-profit making members clubs just now comes from the Justices' Clerks Society. This august body have prepared a secret report which will no doubt, be guided through the proper channels aiming to reach the Statute Book.

I quote............Page four..................

Registered Clubs

"Applications for registration certificates under the Licensing Act, 1964, should be abolished and replaced by an application for a justices' licence with conditions which are designed for a members' club. This is the method favoured by the Justices' Clerks' Society"

It goes on to demand the right of police entry into non profit making members clubs and I quote, for "GENERAL INSPECTION AND SUPERVISORY PURPOSES", what a lovely phrase. It is sometimes claimed that if we have nothing to hide why do we object to the right of police entry? The answer to which is the same reason why we object to the right of police entry into our homes. Police authorities, Justices' Clerks,' Magistrates and local authorities are attempting to make laws without regard to Parliament. Some of you may think we are being paranoiac but we have ample evidence. No doubt they hope to eventually achieve the blessing of Parliament through this report and its recommendations. If enacted, these proposals would destroy the work of millions of people over many years, disrupt their simple leisure time, undermine democracy, feed crime and disorder and be welcomed by "Big Brother", IT MUST BE KILLED.

It is hoped therefore that to resist these attacks and in an endeavour to remedy the situation, you will form this 'All Party Parliamentary Committee' for the protection of the interests of non-profit making members clubs. In turn we, the Club and Institute Union – have formed a sub-committee to inform you of existing problems and pending difficulties which we feel may be resolved in Parliament. We propose to invite onto our Committee, Representatives of the other organisations of clubs which embrace our fundamental principles. In this way we will cover a wide spectrum of opinion and will feel confident that our friends can be more readily recognised in Parliament, more easily contacted and organised in a democratic way for this very worthy purpose.

This speech was received in a very friendly manner and I felt encouraged and confident to go on with the proposal which I had outlined.

The formation of the group excited me more than a little and the enthusiasm shown in Westminster was most encouraging. Soon the group began to grow ultimately reaching more than two hundred. One vexatious issue confronting the Union at that time was the attitude of the Police in seeking harsher regulations to be imposed on clubs applying for registration. The group therefore almost at the beginning of its existence invited the President, Vice President and Secretary of the very influential Association of Chief of Police Officers to a meeting in the House. These gentlemen were forced by Carol Goddard to sign a book which the Union had decided to keep so that attendances at all functions of the group were recorded. The Association of Police Officers people were not impressed; they were even less impressed when they discovered the purpose of their summons. Even so they were informed in no uncertain terms that Parliament would not tolerate any attempts by them to make their own law. Arising from this the Union took up negotiations with the Justices Clerks Society as many complaints had been received by us regarding some unusual and strange interpretations of Licensing Law by some of its members advising Magistrates.

A very friendly understanding and co-operative relationship developed between the CIU and the Justices Clerks Society. We were in regular communication, we had numerous meetings often over a meal either at their Head Quarters in Bristol or ours. We joined forces in outlining new guidelines for their members and Magistrates alike. After a year or two of this extremely useful activity the relationship was severed almost without trace. I understand the reason was that the Council of the Justices Clerk Society believed the CIU and the Justices Clerks Society officials were beginning to get too close and therefore stopped any future joint efforts to conform to and apply the law. At least much good had been done and more could have been. Fortunately we did not have any more cases like the Torbay Magistrates who applied a condition on a Registration Certificate to the effect that persons under eighteen could not consume intoxicates on a club premises. There was no authority vested in these Magistrates by Law to do such a thing. The CIU naturally took the matter to the High Court which instructed the Magistrates to remove their condition at some considerable cost to someone, but not us.

The second issue occupying our minds when the group started was a decision by the Chief Registrar that in future no club registered under the FSA would be permitted to have the Secretary carry out the duty of Treasurer. The law clearly indicated which officers could and could not hold the joint position of Treasurer but it did not specify that the Secretary could not be Treasurer.

Unfortunately when the Chief Registrar made his ruling the General Secretary Frank Morris printed it as a fact in the Club Journal. I was incensed that our General Secretary could so eagerly cave in and felt this must be some form of ingratiating behaviour. I was further alarmed eighteen months later when the new General Secretary Jack Johnson published the same ruling. At the earliest opportunity I raised the question with the Parliamentary group which resolved to seek from the Chief Registrar under what authority or statute he made his ruling. Of course I knew he did not have one, and he was compelled by the group to unceremoniously withdraw it.

By now I and Carol Goddard were getting into the habit of visiting Westminster almost weekly. In this way we got to know numerous members of the House and one or two well known older men who had moved "upstairs" as they say to the Lords. These included Lord Elfed Davis who had been Parliamentary Private Secretary to Harold Wilson and a member of the Board of Directors of our South Wales Brewery. His bosom pal was Lord Blyton of South Shields a life time club man and we became firm friends. When July 1984 arrived I had the shock of a life time as Carol Goddard and I were walking down the steps for the last time that summer we were joined by Gordon Bagier who said "you will be giving a Reception at the Party Conference won't you? We said "of course" although we had not the slightest idea what he meant. Still we had about ten weeks before the Labour Party convened in Blackpool. We quickly discovered what was expected. We made arrangements for a Reception at the Imperial Hotel which was very poorly attended. We were greatly assisted by Lord Brooks of Tremorfa and supported that evening by Gordon Bagier, Mick Welsh, Chairman and Treasurer of the group and his very good friend the Deputy Speaker Harold Walker, later Sir Harold, and now Lord Walker. There were a few more members possibly fifteen, we had catered for seventy-five and naturally were somewhat ridiculed by our colleagues on the Club Union Parliamentary Committee. Over the years from then on we have been responsible for organising Receptions at the Labour Party, the Conservative Party and the Lib-Dem Party Conferences. Almost without exception since the first debacle they have been outstandingly successful and the CIU built up a real reputation in this regard.

From the introduction of the Betting and Lotteries Act of 1934 it had been illegal to play Bingo, Tombola, Housey Housey or Lotto whatever the game was called, it was unlawful. The Union explained that and made it clear to clubs and as far as I was aware no clubs attempted to play. However during the second world war troops in army NAAFI's, seaman on Her Majesty's ships and airmen in hangers often had organised bingo sessions which they thoroughly enjoyed. In the early Fifties many ex-servicemen members, wished to introduce this past-time into their social clubs.

Eventually, due to the insistence and determination of the Union General Secretary, Mr. Frank Castle, who incidentally had been in the Royal Flying Corp in the First World War, the government passed a new Act entitled the Small Lotteries and Gaming Act of 1956 and under the terms of this legislation, it was now possible for clubs to play bingo. There were two separate methods of doing so lawfully. One was to play what was known as Section 40, which was bingo as a gaming activity and the other method was to play the game as an entertainment. This second method was under Section 41 and it did entail much stricter control in that only one payment for tickets by any one person could be made in any one day, only one distribution of prizes could be made in any one day and the stakes were strictly limited as were the prizes. All the profits thus made had to be devoted to the purposes of the club.

Most clubs took up this opportunity to play under one or other of the sections which the law permitted. However the Huddersfield Friendly & Trades Club in 1960 was prosecuted and the officers of the club were convicted for playing tombola as an entertainment under Section 41 of the Act. The Magistrates held that as the net proceeds of the entertainment were devoted to the payment of the general expenses of the club and providing the amenities for members this constituted "private gain". Accordingly the Magistrates held that the entertainment was an unlawful lottery and not exempt under Section 40. This action was brought to the notice of the Union Executive who resolved that the Union would finance an appeal against the Magistrate's findings.

It is interesting to note that when the Union appealed to the Lord Chief Justice in regard to the Huddersfield Friendly and Trades Society Club's case, the LCJ held against the club. It was decided therefore that an application be made for leave to appeal to the House of Lords against this judgement. The court granted that the application should proceed. The Petition of the appeal was lodged at the House of Lords for the hearing to be held on the 4th May.

Eventually judgement from the House of Lords was delivered on the 23rd June, and by a majority of 3-2 the law lords found against the club and dismissed the appeal with costs. The Union took immediate steps to seek a meeting with the Rt. Hon. R.A. Butler and the new Secretary of State at the Home Office Mr. David Renton, QC MP who had agreed to meet a deputation from the Union on the 4th July at the House of Commons in order to discuss the effect of this Judgement and the possibility of amending the legislation. The terms of a reply by Mr. Renton in the House of Commons on 3rd August indicated that the Government were examining the position and the possible ways in which the law might be amended.

At a National Executive meeting in December 1961 it was reported that Mr. John C. Bidgood, MP being No. 10 in the draw for Private Members' Bills had tabled a Bill with respect to the interpretation on reference to Private Gain as used in the Acts relating to Betting, Gaming and Lotteries, and that such Bill was due to be read a second time on 23rd March. It was reported that from information obtained, being No. 10 in the draw, there was little likelihood of the Bill becoming Law.

The General Secretary reported on the terms of a further letter to Mr. D. Renton QC, MP Minister of State at the Home Office in which he again asked for an early appointment with the Home Secretary or the Minister of State in order to discuss the position of Private Gain which was becoming more confused every day, and whilst a reply had been received from Mr. Renton's Private Secretary, he did not indicate his agreement to meet a deputation.

It was then resolved by the Union National Executive Committee that the General Secretary continue to request a meeting with a view to pressing for early legislation to clarify the position.

Under section 40, playing as an activity, the reverse applied as the law insisted that every penny taken for the purchase of bingo tickets had to be returned to the player by way of prizes. Nothing could be kept back which really made Snowballs impossible to develop. The club had to charge an entrance fee in order to defray its costs, e.g. the printing of the actual tickets.

In 1962 Blaina Working Men's and Ebbw Vale Working Men's clubs were both prosecuted after police took proceedings against these clubs for having a snowball at their Tombola sessions. The

Union reprimanded the clubs for breaking the law, but then sought to obtain an amendment to the law so that clubs could again introduce this practise which could have been very popular. Because bingo now had spread throughout Britain, the commercial interests set up bingo halls around the country to play on a profit making basis. The Government encouraged this and saw a way of obtaining revenue therefore to take part in the playing of Bingo it was decreed that a tax of 10% be levied on the sale of all tickets.

The Government was not slow to recognise the fiscal value of any past-time as popular as this. So before long Bingo Tax was introduced at ten percent of the stakes but it only applied to the commercial operators. They quickly formed themselves into a protective organisation known as the Bingo Association of Great Britain (BAGB) this organisation felt they were unfairly treated on the tax issue when we were, in the non-profit making sector exempted. Their lobby continually pressed the Government to place the tax upon our form of Bingo. Eventually in the middle of the night when the Government had been persuaded by the farmers to reduce fuel tax on some diesel, it was decided that the shortfall should be made up by a tax on non-profit Bingo.

This caused dismay in the CIU and other non-profit making Clubs. It was necessary now to maintain complex records. At the same time a considerable amount of money was being collected for the Government. It was not unusual for Customs officials when inspecting club's Bingo records to discover shortfall payments of three thousand pounds or more. For these reasons I found myself at loggerheads with BAGB who were as it happened particularly pleasant people and their Consultant in Parliament was my own MP Sir Peter Fry who was too much of a gentlemen and too intelligent and educated to allow the situation between the CIU and BAGB to deteriorate and we always stayed friends. However my determination to abolish Bingo duty was not affected. My arguments were straight forward and it was the difference between profit making and non-profit making.

I knew that BAGB wanted a change in the law to allow them to advertise and made it clear that as long as we paid Bingo duty I would remain hell-bent on asking the Parliamentary group to prevent them from advertising. By now Greg Knight who had followed Barry Porter as the Conservative Chairman of the group had been appointed a Government Whip and his place was taken by John Watts as the Conservative Chairman. John Watts a Cambridge graduate and also a Chartered Accountant and member for Slough had an excellent reputation among his colleagues not least in financial matters. Therefore he was almost always a member of Finance Committees dealing with the budgets as they came along. With a little prompting from the group and through Parliamentary questions I obtained information from Customs and Excise. One evening John Watts submitted an amendment, which I had written, to the Finance Bill which was carried by his Tory colleagues supported by Labour and Liberal alike which had the desired effect of abolishing Bingo duty in the non-profit making sector. This change in the Finance Bill cost the Government seventy million pounds per year, of which thirty million pounds was a saving for CIU clubs alone. The remaining forty million pounds spread around the other members of CORCA.

I wrote the motion to do this on a serviette in the Strangers refreshment room of the House of Commons gave it to John who submitted it that evening at the committee. I, together with Carol Goddard, my secretary, sat outside the room where the debate was proceeding regarding the Finance Bill. Before the evening was out, we received the news from John that the committee had accepted my motion that the duty be abolished for non-profit making members clubs.

We then withdraw any opposition against BAGBs desire to advertise and joined forces with them and to some extent with the British Casino Association in our negotiation with the Government for a more relaxed approach to gaming machines. The Casino Association impressed by the work of our group were anxious to work with us in the pursuit of some of their objectives. Before long we were having tri-party meetings, Casino Association, BAGB and CIU which were frequently attended by Richard Alexander who was something of an expert in racing circles, Sir Peter Fry and others. The BAGB and the Casinos wanted four gaming machines, the CIU and CORCA wanted three. In the case of BAGB they seldom used gaming machines as the Law did not allow gaming machines and amusements with prizes (AWP) to be on the same premises. In the Bingo halls they needed lots of machines and therefore elected for AWP and the numbers allowed at each venue being determined by the local Magistrates. The Government repeatedly refused to increase the numbers of gaming machines anywhere.

One day I was being entertained in the Harcourt Room, later to be known as the Churchill Room, by a couple of MPs when I was shown a simple amendment Bill designed to give the casinos four machines. It reaffirmed two in registered clubs and two for BAGB, "what would you like us to do" I was asked. I said immediately "the Union will go for three" MPs clustered around to decide how to use the procedures of the House to hold the Bill up long enough for them to amend it. They even went to the point of deciding which among their names would serve on the Committee of the Bill. Within half an hour everything was in motion. Sometimes people think Parliament works slowly I can vouch that is not always true! Two minutes later Sir Peter Fry was at the table demanding to know what I had done and claiming if we had three he wanted three. So I said I didn't mind what you had Peter, I could not speak for you anyway. Peter knew the procedure as well as anyone and wanted to put his three in. The Bill went through a number of stages including the Committee and came before the House for the third reading. The Government had resolved to kill the Bill in its amended form which meant everything was lost. Anglea Rombold was the Minister from the Home Office from 10th May 1991 and in explaining why the Government rejected the amended Bill she said it would probably have been safe and right to allow the casinos to have four machines but there was no case for Working Men's Clubs and the like to go from two to three. At this point Mr. Dennis Skinner who did not seem to support lobby groups asked the Minister if that kind of reasoning was what the Government meant by a classless society. From then on the Casino Association who had worked closely with us became a little distant and felt somewhat let down. However later on fences were mended and the CIU and the Casino Association were friends once more. They got their machines, we got ours and BAGB got theirs.

Back Row/ Kevin Smythe, Alan Beith, Brian Winters.
Front Row/ Lord Brooks, Derek Dormer and
NE Branch President

NEC, at Langland Convalesecent Home

The Dormer Family

Derek and family going to a garden party
at Buckingham Palace

Playing my piano

Linda, Derek, Gladys and Thomas

Gladys Dormer

Gladys and Derek Dormer

At the Speakers House, Palace of Westminster

Blackpool

Performing Rights Society – For many years the Club Union was almost obsessed with the entire Performing Rights Society subject. One simple way of gaining popularity among the delegates at Conference was to mount the rostrum and criticise firstly the PRS and secondly the NEC for letting them get away with it. Every club had paid their fees and few seemed to understand the justification. Having paid the band, or brought the record, it was difficult to follow the logic of paying a duty on a piece of sheet music say, every time it was played, if the club actually owned it. As a consequence the PRS had great difficulty in collecting what was due as clubs refused generally to co-operate. The CIU as I have said earlier being virtually obsessed with conforming to the law it did not necessarily agree with the copyright law which protected the PRS and its members, be it composers, arrangers or publishers. For this reason it was felt in exchange for due consideration by which I mean a small discount payable to the Union itself then we would assist the PRS to collect from our clubs. To do this we simply made the case and explained the law encouraging clubs to meet these demands. Then, it was the vexed issue of the tariff under which clubs were assessed for the amount due. Naturally this varied a great deal from club to club. Every year the PRS sought to increase the tariff so as to enlarge its revenue for distribution. I understand that approximately ninety percent of the PRS income is distributed to approximately five percent of its members. This does not help to endear them to the CIU membership. The rows between us and the PRS over the tariff became more and more heated.

Under the Copyright Act the Performing Rights Society had the power to charge for the use of their members' work when performed in public. Although members clubs are not strictly speaking public places, it had been conceded that the Performing Rights Society did have a case to charge for their members' work when performing at club functions. Rather than having a separate fee for individual songs, the Union had negotiated an overall annual licence to cover Working Men's Clubs. In 1962 the Performing Rights Society asked that the annual fee be increased to seven pounds seven shillings per year. The Union President, Ted McEnery, and General Secretary negotiated with the Society and it was agreed that the annual fee for Working Men's Clubs to pay the Performing Rights Society from 1962,`63 and `64 would be six pound and six shillings per year which would give the clubs authority to play any music whether copyright or not.

This arrangement carried on and from time to time negotiations took place to increase the fees accordingly. What was unknown to the National Executive, Branch Executives and the Union generally was that Head Office of the CIU received a commission from all these fees paid by the clubs.

This fact was only revealed when Bernard Holleworth the Secretary and National Executive representative for Derbyshire asked a pertinent question on the annual accounts as to the make-up of the item headed commissions. Because of Bernard's persistence the General Secretary was compelled to divulge the fact that part of the commission shown in the annual accounts was from the Performing Rights Society. The National Executive Committee, on hearing this information were aghast as there had always been animosity between the Union and the Performing Rights Society. To placate the National Executive it was agreed that the Branches would now receive a share of this commission.
In the summer of 1962 the Performing Rights Society circulated all Union clubs asking them to complete an Annual Return for the year ended 5th August 1962. The form asked for many and various details including matters relating to musical and other activities such as Tombola. This form had been circulated to all Union clubs without any prior consultation or discussion with the Union whatsoever. At its meeting in August 1962 the National Executive was livid and instructed the President and General Secretary to seek an immediate interview with the General Management of the Society and in the meantime Union clubs were circulated to the effect that the return should not be completed. During the next few weeks the Union Officers successfully persuaded the Performing Rights Society not to pursue their request, but that a simplified form be sent to each club and the club would pay a fee in accordance with the agreement which had been reached earlier in the year.

However we refused to accept any settlement for the new tariff. In doing this it was our task to seek a ruling from the copyright tribunal. To do so was going to cost about three quarters of a million pounds in legal fees if we won, and twice that if we lost.

The process took nearly three years and in the meantime under the law as it then existed our clubs were obliged to pay at the new disputed rate. Because of this the PRS in its anger dropped the commission payments to us from ten to seven percent, but continued to pay ten percent to the Association of Conservative Clubs who did not join in our battle as other sectors did.

We made an appeal to our clubs for a fighting fund to ease our financial commitment. The clubs in our Union, to their everlasting credit, contributed £300,000.00. Another indication of their feelings against the PRS.

We won. Hands Down. The Chairman quite reasonably and logically explained that "as much as the existing tariff was based on fees paid to Artists and other entitlement costs then because of inflation the PRS was receiving an increase every year without any effort and therefore no reasonable case had been made out.

He ordered that all the additional fees paid over the last three years was to be re-paid. The PRS met us to endeavour to find a way of re-distributing the money they had grabbed so quickly whilst the case was pending. Their computer system could not handle it so I volunteered to do it for them if we agreed on a global figure based on information we both had. I sought to take one million pounds more than the global figure indicated. Present with them were several lawyers and accountants, they paid the figure asked for and the extra million was fed over a five year period into the Branch Secretaries' Pension Fund which I had established two or three years earlier.

Then to come back to Parliament the Government decided to have a new Copyright Act. Jack Johnson being something of an expert in these matters studied its content. Jack conceived the idea of changing the system which applied when tariffs were disputed or new ones not agreed. Jack devised a plan which meant that in future if the PRS wished to increase their tariff and it was disputed by the user, such as the CIU, then under the proposed amendment to the new law it was to become the responsibility of the PRS to appeal to a tribunal and make its case and not the other way around as hitherto. This plan in proper Parliamentary language was submitted to the Government at a late stage in passage of the latest Copyright Bill on almost the last day in July that Parliament was sitting, the Copyright Bill was receiving its final examination by the Copyright Parliamentary Committee. The Minister in charge for the Government was John Butcher from Coventry. He came to me on the terrace at the House and said "Derek you have got your Copyright amendment and you have Betty Boothroyd to thank for "it". I knew what he meant; Betty was Chairman of the Parliamentary Committee on the Bill, although she was not on the Government bench. She was an expert in procedures and it was through her careful conduct over the proceedings that this amendment got through. Strangely enough ten minutes after John Butcher gave me the information, I was elated and delighted and even more pleased when Betty came along. I stood up to greet her as I always did and said "thank you Betty for what you did today" she replied "I have no idea what you are talking about."

In the year 2001 the PRS had not paid any commission due for the previous year and threatened to dispose of the assistance of the CIU in collecting its fees which of course is a back door method of increasing them.

In 1977 a young man from Northampton, Kevin Smyth was appointed the new Union's Education Secretary. He was very popular and thoroughly enjoyed his work in organising a massive education programme throughout the Union. Fifteen years later in September 1992 as Jack Johnson was preparing to retire as General Secretary, Kevin Smyth sought election and was overwhelmingly elected. He assumed office as the General Secretary on the 12th October that year. Kevin and I worked closely together although our backgrounds were very different we did understand one another's approach and I believe this worked to the benefit of the movement.

Gradually Carol Goddard and myself developed a routine of visiting the House of Commons at least once a week. Making friends, listening to what was going on, trying to understand the procedures. Earlier on when it was obvious what our objectives seemed to be we were getting great help, from Jack Dormond MP for Easington, later to become Lord Dormond. Jack was born in a Working Men's Club and he was a man of the highest integrity and principles. He had been a member of a select committee charged with the task of regulating special interest groups and lobby activities in the Palace of Westminster. It had just produced a blue pamphlet on their work which had been accepted by the Government. Jack got me a copy as soon as it was available and as a consequence Carol Goddard and I studied the content minutely and became quite experts on the things that lobby groups could and could not do. Although it may sound somewhat boastful we quickly realised that we knew more about these procedures than almost any MP. This enabled us to ensure that the All Party Parliamentary Group in the interests of non-profit making Members Clubs would be correctly organised.

One day when we were waiting in the Central Lobby for an MP with whom we had pre-arranged to collect us we were noticed by Ray Powell, now Sir Raymond. He was an active member of the group. He was also the Labour pairing whip and because of this he had some special power. As the Government parties had many more members obviously than the opposition, it meant there were not enough pairs for many of the junior Conservative Members. Many of them found it necessary to always be in the precinct of the Palace. We were able through our influence, from time to time, to persuade the opposition whip to find a pair for those junior Government MPs who were active in the group.

One evening I travelled to Westminster in something of an agitated state of mind. For several weeks Parliament had been debating a Bill entitled Scottish (Miscellaneous) Provisions Amendment Bill, which was being piloted through the Commons by Malcolm Rifkin, then Secretary of State for Scotland. In its provisions there was a Clause which gave power to the Police to enter upon club premises at any time, in or out of uniform, in any number, without prior notification and without a warrant. The exact purpose of such intrusions was not really properly set out. I was very fearful that if this measure went through Parliament it would not be long before the same thing happened to England and Wales.

Wandering about the House that evening alone, I had reached a state of desperation. Suddenly and fortuitously in a yard between the buildings I came face to face with Marcus Fox later Sir Marcus who at the time was the Chairman of the Conservative 1922 Committee. This committee has always been influential as it is comprised of all Conservative MP's who are not members of the Government or the Shadow Government. He was also President of the Association of Conservative clubs, a member of the group and MP for Shipley. I pleaded with him to obtain for me an interview with the Prime Minster Mrs. Thatcher, he enquired why I was so concerned and when I told him he gave me a knowing wink and re-assured me that he would deal with the matter. Two days later the measure was withdrawn. Malcolm Rifkin was reported as saying he could not understand what all the fuss was about, two days after that I saw Marcus at the other end of the bar and he gave me that knowing wink again with his thumbs up and he knew how delighted I was with his efforts.

The Police have an obsession it seems to intrude on peoples' lives in their private surroundings. They find it difficult to think that men and women and their families are able to resort to a private place, to sing and dance, play games, talk, debate, have some refreshments, perhaps a smoke without supervision. Private Members Clubs have their own well tried and tested codes of discipline. There are proper procedures which are adhered to when members are alleged to have committed an offence. These procedures are over-ridden if a criminal offence having occurred outside any club is proved in a court of law. A private members club is in many cases an extension of the family. The less authority have to do with it the better yet police forces still keep trying.

In January in the year 2000 the Home Office issued proposals once again containing a clause in a new Licensing Bill to give police the right of access. This would mean the right to overrun a club, frightening many people, young and old for no real purposes. When Kevin Smyth and I first became aware of this suggestion we immediately took the matter to Lord Jack Brooks the Secretary of the group. He wrote to the Minister concerned, Mike O'Brien with whom he later spoke. Kevin and myself met with officials from the Home Office and we met them again with the Minister. We made it crystal clear that working people particularly would resent any police presence.

I was informed that the Home Secretary, Jack Straw, was concerned to know what the club movement thought on this point. He was told in no uncertain terms. To their everlasting credit Mike O'Brien no doubt with Jack Straw's blessing withdrew the proposal. Almost certainly, although I have no evidence, the idea originated through the Association of Chief of Police Officers. They could not have been very happy when they learned that the clause was once again eliminated. Although I have no proof I am certain in my own mind that upon enquiring in the Home Office or perhaps even by deduction they discovered the reason for their plan being destroyed. It may well be they saw names and if they did my own would certainly have been revealed. People may think its pure imagination but in July of 2000 just a couple of months after this withdrawal I was harassed by senior police officers which continued for seven or eight months during which time I was breathalysed many times, pursued for ten miles at night and threatened with being arrested at least three times. As it happened my record, whilst writing this is still unblemished. In fact the continual breathalysing did not end until the year 2004 when I changed my car.

Convalescent Homes

The big moment in the lives of active club men, not so much women, but men who serve as Officers or Committee Men in Working Men's Clubs is the annual trip to Blackpool. On my first visit in March 1950 about four hundred men assembled to hear the President's address followed by two short addresses from the local MPs and then a longer talk by a Government or Institution Official always preceded by a welcome from the Mayor. The afternoon session was attended by about six hundred delegates who had been travelling that morning, mostly from Lancashire and Yorkshire. The session devoted itself almost entirely to a study of the Union's Annual Report. Usually there were really good speeches from the floor, and quite a lot of criticism and much resentment if there was the slightest attack by the NEC on any Government proposals. I got the impression that most delegates were also strong Labour supporters. As time went by the attendances at the Conferences grew, so by around 1970 the figure of delegates applying had risen to about two thousand six hundred and on occasion there were attendances of up to two thousand four hundred delegates. The work of the Union had also developed and I began to feel that as so many people wished to speak we would find difficulty in completing the business in one day.

Meetings were lasting until six o'clock in the evening whereas our time was put at five o'clock. I realised that a great deal of the time was taken up by arguments over procedure. About 1975/6 just before the meeting came to order at ten o'clock in the morning I thought it would be a help to have a Standing Orders Committee to deal with issues of procedure away from the main meeting. I asked Arthur Bates' permission, he agreed and I put to the Conference that four members of the NEC who were Chairmen of Sub Committees would form a Standing Orders Committee. I worked out some rough rules as I spoke and this was accepted. It has developed over the years and has proved to be very useful indeed. Many people in club life used to spend six months talking about last year's Conference and the next six months talking about the Conference to come. It was such an event that the Executive felt the need to try to bring all delegates together for a social occasion under one roof. As it happened in the fifties the Scottish Branch I believe initiated a Queen of Clubs Competition. Beauty pageants had become popular in holiday resorts and the Miss World competition was on the TV. Pictures were being published of these young ladies in the Journal and other Branches in the Union took up the challenge. The Union Executive therefore decided if the Branches could have a Queen of Clubs and at that stage twenty-six of thirty did, there was a good case for having a National Queen of Clubs. The Branch winners were the only competitors allowed. It was held in the Empress Ballroom after the Conference and was expertly organised by Peter Miller the Recreation Secretary. Incidentally he was never short of helpers for this job from the Recreation Committee. Some contestants were also well organised bringing supporters by the bus load from their local area. My wife and I had a great time being photographed whilst presenting the prizes to the winners and consolation boxes to the losers. By the end of the eighties the idea of young ladies parading themselves, all be it in beautiful clothes and the latest hairdos, became politically incorrect. I think this was a pity although in a way I was not too disappointed because at the last one or two national contests there was an element of yobbish behaviour from one or two clubs supporting their local girls. During its very popular period some Branches actually organised a glamorous Grandmother contest, but I thought this was going a bit too far.

Work As Union President

In 1972 the Government issued a White Paper designed to form the basis of the legislation for VAT. I obtained a copy of this document, and a day or so after on 31st October 1972 I was due to give a lecture in Leeds. I left my car at Peterborough station and in the two hours it then took to travel to Leeds I read, re-read, studied and thought about its contents. I realised that very few of the Secretaries of the clubs whom I knew, would be able to master the complexity of VAT. In principal VAT is a simple concept. But, in the case of Private Social Clubs which then had gaming machines there would need to be a special formula applied to determine the amount of tax due. The reason for this was that all forms of gaming were exempt. This included raffles, totes, bingo and of course the main source gaming machines. Because the total income, referred to as outputs, relating to gaming broke a certain percentage of the total, a smaller percentage of inputs to outputs was permitted to be re-claimed. The difficulties this formula presented were in my opinion insurmountable for many clubs. This happened in the Autumn around October and the tax was to begin on 1st April 1973. I resolved to write a computer programme to make the necessary returns for clubs. At the same time by computer I would produce most of the secondary books of accounts. I set about the task and in the December of that year invited the computer expert and another supervisor of the Inland Revenue to inspect a sample of the work my programme produced both technically and for accuracy. I invited them to criticise the finished product. They took the sample and the software away, returning just before Christmas to tell me that it all worked perfectly. I asked if they would give me a letter to that effect but they could not do so. We then, through D.J.Dormer & Son Limited set about marketing the scheme. Before April 1st we had about one hundred and fifty clubs signed up. I was pressed to go nationwide but did not want to.

By about June/July I was having severe problems with the programme as it kept losing the headers. I was ready to throw it all in and withdraw the service. I told Leslie Tillotson the Data Processing Manager at John Whites that I could not solve the programme problem. He produced a young lady named Diana McKinley who put it right in no time. While all this was going on the Union was much concerned to teach clubs how to account for VAT. Jack Johnson, myself and others toured the country to give lectures on the system. We had high audiences wherever we went through the autumn and winter of 1971/72. The Union published a booklet which is still available. Personally I did not agree with the Union's official system that was based on keeping a register of invoices received from which to claim the input tax whereas the system which I favoured was to claim inputs after the invoices had been paid. I felt this was a safer way because there was least likelihood of missing any input claims. The one drawback to my system was that one month's inputs were claimed later than they could have been.

So far as Customs and Excise were concerned both systems were acceptable. I did not agree either with the ruling that Ashley Waker had devised for the Unions number one cash book. He had a column on the receipt side for VAT which I believed demonstrated that he did not understand the tax. This led to severe arguments for a long time. After about five years the Government in a Finance Bill, decided that although all gaming activities were exempt from VAT there was to be an exemption to the exempts and that was gaming machines. This meant that the complexities in the partial exempt status which clubs enjoyed would be no longer acceptable as the limits of exempt outputs the percentage would not be reached or hardly ever.

When I joined the Union Executive in 1954 there were five convalescent homes, the most recent was the conversion of a great mansion in Nantwich, Cheshire. The Union purchased the building and the very extensive grounds, it was in a beautiful setting. A great deal of money was spent in decorating and furnishing the interior. It was the first home I had visited and it was valued for the quality and surroundings, inside and out. The other four homes were at the seaside and this one being relatively near Crewe was little used for the reason that many people felt that the seaside was necessary for convalescing. At the time there was a great deal of sickness mainly among the pit-men and men working in heavy industry, recovering often from hernias. The miners suffered all kinds of respiratory illness. Most of them were still living in poor back to back terraced housing and a stay at a convalescent home by the seaside with plenty of food, warmth, rest and fresh air was invaluable. After two or three years it was obvious that Nantwich had to be sold. A very glossy brochure was produced and circulated by the agents. Few people showed interest and rumours began that the building had dry rot. Oscar Snelson member of the Executive from North Staffs and South Cheshire, and President of the Branch was given virtual plenary power to sell the property. In the end we received six thousand pounds which was a severe disappointment. As far as I know the building was eventually pulled down and a housing estate erected on the site. Next to go was Pegwell Bay which had been given to the Union in 1894. In 1967 there was a great flood in the area and the house which had three floors above the cliff and two floors below, was flooded to almost destruction. The sea came up to the home and rushed the five floors of the lift, flooding every room in the building. Pegwell contained some of the Unions treasures and most valuable possessions. No real paper record was kept, but it was general knowledge that some of the pictures were virtually in the priceless bracket. These disappeared, some said they were taken across the Channel and many rumours ensued – but it was no rumour that Interpol were called in by the Kent police to investigate. At least one member of the staff was arrested but later released. There was a big insurance settlement but no-one, as far as I know saw the details. I believe the pictures were not included as the value was unknown. In place of Pegwell we built Broadstairs home.

The Union President laid the foundation stone and the building was opened in July 1971 by Doctor Horace King, at that time Speaker of the House of Commons and later Lord Mawbray King originally Member of Parliament for Southampton Test and a great friend to the Union to the end of his days. As the nation's health and housing improved and jobs were becoming safer through health and safety regulations, the need for convalescence declined. The Union Executive were aware for several years that four homes were unnecessary and it was impossible to justify their continued operation. Much thought was given to disposing of one of them and the Executive decided upon Grange-Over-Sands for a number of reasons. It stood in a most prominent position and had been built specially by the Union and completed just before the First World War. It was immediately taken over by the military as a hospital but handed back to the Union on 7th August 1916. The decision to dispose of Grange caused much resentment particularly among the clubs in the North West of England. Even so the facts were irrefutable and among other things revealed that club men even from Cumbria did not use the home, only seven from that Branch had been resident in the whole year prior to the decision. The Executive went ahead and disposed of it with great reluctance but without any option in 1989.

In the early 1990's it began to appear that the three remaining homes were not being used to the full by any means. Ideas came from all quarters for extending and broadening the use of the homes. The Education Department was anxious to use the facilities for various types of weekend schools. Some open to any of our members, others for special Branch Secretaries and CMD students or club Secretaries. These weekend uses of the homes were nearly all very successful. In the overall context of the number of beds available in the three homes in the first year the use made by the Education Committee contributed very little indeed. In fact it is doubtful whether there was a net financial contribution to the Union in this way.

It became inevitable that a decision especially in the finance committee would turn to the disposal of yet another of our homes. Soon members of the Executive began to fall into different camps, Saltburn, Broadstairs and Langland. Strong arguments were advanced about each of the individual homes. Among those who accepted that it was time for at least one to be sold a view became fairly established that we should retain one home for the North and one for the South. This argument of course safeguarded Saltburn which in many ways was the poorest equipped of the three. But it certainly helped to bring a majority of the Executive to the only conclusion available, one must go. Therefore the issue settled on the preference between Langland and Broadstairs. All aspects about the decision were thrashed out time after time and although Broadstairs was the newest and purposely built in recent years the argument settled on retaining Langland particularly as some development had taken place internally to provide en-suite bedrooms which Broadstairs did not have. When the decision was finally and irrevocably made a great storm of protest erupted. That year it was decided by the Executive to call a special meeting of the Union to explain the reasons for the sale of Broadstairs and to consider changing the Union's rules regarding Section 49 of the Licensing Act 1964. The special meeting was held at Wellingborough British Railway Sports & Social Club, It was a terrifying experience and I think that I failed to hold the meeting as well as I should have done, certainly not as well as McEnery had in the famous meeting in Leicester regarding the change of name. There were extenuating circumstances. The club is enormous in size and very well managed, there were one thousand people in the main hall. I had a dreadful shock when I found the stage microphone did not work but the speaker's microphone on the floor did. The meeting was virtually out of control. I had an idiotic situation of trying to chair a meeting, and in order to make myself heard asking to borrow the speaker's microphone. The principle attack against the National Executive was lead by Allan Lavelle who later became President of Northumberland and member of the NEC. Alan was quite ruthless and gave no quarter and showed no mercy in rubbishing the NEC. He was cheered all the way and the Union Executive and myself were very hurt by the reaction of the delegates. However, the decision to sell Broadstairs had been made and there was no power vested in that meeting to reverse that action.

The second question was the consideration of changing the ruling of the Union to allow a Section 49 amendment in Union clubs. This part of the Licensing Act of 1964 allows clubs in certain circumstance to sell intoxicants to members of the public, for example when the club rents off some part of its premises for weddings and the like. My view and that of most of the Executive was that this dispensation was really intended by Parliament for those private registered clubs which were not members of any association. It should be remembered that until 1964 there was no statute in existence which gave any legal standing to the Unions' Associate Card. By doing so it created the position where by a club could lawfully sell intoxicants to any associate member. Section 49 therefore was not required by Union clubs.

Nevertheless the British Legion Clubs, Conservative Clubs and others had adopted this Section. The Union's view was strongly against, in fact the rules of the Union provides should any club adopt this section then it can no longer remain in membership. The Union explained time and time again that if Section 49 was adopted then the police would have right of entry, it is doubtful whether gaming machines would continue to be used lawfully on the premises and thirdly there would certainly be a tax on the profit on any sale or transaction between the club and public, although attempts by different individuals to persuade the Executive to change its view were defeated. The principle advocate of Section 49 in the Union was Keith Barrowcliffe JP who being a Magistrate was fairly well versed in these matters. Most people considered his opinions were a little suspect but he was relentless. In the end I rather lost my cool with Keith and from the chair admonished him severely with the comment that I never wanted to hear Section 49 mentioned again in a Union Executive meeting. This had the desired effect, for a couple of years nothing was said. During those two years I began to realise that if so many clubs in the country had adopted Section 49 and got away with it we needed to perhaps think again. But over and above that I knew there was approximately two hundred British Legion clubs which were also members of the CIU and almost certainly they had Section 49. I wrestled with the problem of knowing that some two hundred clubs were breaking the Union rules without censure. This was an impossible position and so I changed my mind. I decided to put it to the Executive that the time had arrived when we should give clubs an opportunity to change the Union rules, so that those clubs who wished, as long as they knew the risk, could adopt Section 49. Everybody thought Keith had got to me somehow. I didn't think so – but perhaps unconsciously I had taken on board some of his points, but I didn't give him any credit for it. The Executive voted in favour of my proposal and we took the opportunity to submit the motion at the Wellingborough meeting. The delegates threw back our own argument which we had used for so long, and despite the fact that it would have been voluntary, and each club would decide for itself, the motion was lost by a mile. It might have been different in calmer waters. The Wellingborough meeting was a nightmare.

The Union and New Towns

I often used to say that I could remember reading the Club Journal when I was four years old! I certainly started at a very early age and I have always been keen that it should be read widely and be a successful official organ of the CIU. When I became active as a Union Officer in the early fifties, I began to form the opinion that the Journal was used too much to advertise the egos of the Union Officers and staff. When I joined the Union Executive I was surprised to learn that the Journal was not controlled by the

Executive at all. It was run almost entirely by the people who worked in Head Office. Perhaps I should not have been surprised in view of its content. I resolved that ideally the Journal would come under the control of an elected Committee. For starters I wanted to see the Education Committee take it over. All my early attempts were crushed. I believed that it was necessary to mention as many names of ordinary people as possible to keep their interest. (I think what attracted me was each month there would be a Branch report in the Journal). I therefore proposed that, as each month the Union awarded many Certificates of Merit for ten years service and long service awards for twenty-five years that there should be a Roll of Honour and these names would appear as they qualify in the Journal. I was successful in making this demand and it has proved very popular. Later we added the Distinguished Service Awards. Up until that time the Journal only carried names of people in disgrace, expelled or suspended from their clubs. Later on the Union for some reason which I never understood, decided to scrap the report of Branch Council meetings. This was a pity I thought because it again carried the names of local officials and delegates at Branch Council and although I concede there was some repetition in the reports, I thought they were well worthwhile.

On my list of things to do as President was the establishment of a Journal Board, by this time I had more influence for obvious reasons and was supported in this project. John Tobin became at least a member, if not Chairman of the Board and I was not too happy when he decided to change the format from magazine to tabloid. I know that it was not a popular move in the House of Commons where, in its magazine form, I often saw MP's sitting around and some Members of the Lords reading the Journal. It was not often quoted to me after it became like a newspaper and it is very rarely referred to in Westminster. I also think it's more difficult to sell in the clubs, and despite all the advertising it is still expensive. When I was on Wolverton Central Committee in 1951 and 1952, I was the Journal Agent, and sold a gross every month when they were two pence a copy. The Union's main task of course is to spread the word and whereas the three principle methods of disseminating information were through meetings, lectures and the printed word all these sources have been reduced in their effect by the introduction of telephones, television, computers and other modern methods.

I always felt, even at school that I had some ability to address meetings. I went to my first Club Union lecture in December 1947, when Andrew Temple the retired Education Secretary gave a talk on the Union and its Constitution. I was fascinated by what he had to say and absorbed every word. The next year or two as a Branch Secretary, I arranged a day school in the Wolverton area. In those days we always had two lecturers, one in the afternoon and one after tea. I had invited a man named Harrison to talk about the financial depression in clubs. It was an embarrassing experience as most of the people in my Branch who came to listen knew far more than he did. The errors were fundamental and I decided that I would have to become a lecturer myself. The second lecturer that day was Sam Appleyard Chairman of the Union Education Committee and Secretary of the Leeds Branch. He became my mentor for as long as he lived, but that day I asked what I needed to do to become a Union lecturer. Incidentally there were no fees paid to lecturers in those days. He told me to write a précis on the subject I wished to lecture and submit it to him. I had chosen to speak about Chairmanship and Procedure at Meetings which Sam corrected and I was ready to go. The first invitation for me to speak at a Union School came from Bert Rowe and my co-lecturer was Edward McEnery. Bert Rowe was a Chartered Accountant, a high ranking Freemason and Secretary of South Wales Branch and a member of the Union Finance Committee. Why he invited me I shall never know. I travelled to Cardiff and that was the first time I had ever had a meal on a train. McEnery lectured first, they did not have a tea but they did have thirty-six gallons of beer donated by the South Wales and Monmouthshire Clubs Brewery. I was not especially nervous and went onto the stage to deliver my lecture which was supposed to last for one hour. I walked about back and forward, left to right, stuttered and stammered and finally after about twenty-five minutes had no more to say and asked for questions. Those men in that Cardiff Club that day gave me massive encouragement and after the ordeal was over, several came to me with hints and suggestions on how to improve my performance. Members of the Union Executive were anxious to encourage a young man like me and the invitations to speak began to come from all quarters. I established quite a reputation in a very short time. Often I would give a lecture in one town and then move on to another, some way away. I have lectured in every Branch in the Union without exception on a number of occasions, over a fifty year period I must have given at least two thousand lectures. My son Thomas joined the lecture panel around about 1998 and he established a good reputation, he did have a natural ability, he didn't have and hasn't got my knowledge of how clubmen operate. By the year 2001 day lectures are almost a thing of the past, some branches hold lectures on the same day as the Branch Council Meeting but even then with two functions organised at the same time, the numbers barely warrant the costs involved. Originally as I said lecturers received no fee but they were entitled to claim the nominal second class travel allowance and three days and two nights subsistence.

When the expenses rate had increased to six pounds per day John Holmes requested that lecturers be paid a fee, by then John was doing a great number of lectures, probably more than me. The Committee agreed to pay the extra days expenses of six pounds to count as a fee, I pointed out that the six pounds would be taxable but my advice was probably ignored, and I don't suppose I declared it myself at that time. When I became Chairman of the Education Committee I introduced evening schools, here the lecturer received two days and one nights expenses plus the extra six pounds for this fee.

Once being elected Vice President of the Union in 1970 the time had come to move on from Education. Although prior to that I sat on a Committee originally known as the Advisory Committee which met in the middle of the month. It was set up because John Holmes, when he first was elected, made some terrible fundamental basic errors in advising certain clubs on several issues. Two of these letters containing absolute rubbish were received by clubs in the Doncaster Branch. The Doncaster President and member of the Union's Recreation Committee was a colliery man, fair and square and very frank. He raised this issue warning the members at the Union Executive meeting, in a blistering attack on the General Secretary John Holmes. Powerful as McEnery was he found it difficult to protect his protégée against Jack Saxton. McEnery then had an ingenious idea which would get him to London as regularly as he wished. He proposed that all the letters containing legal advice going out from Head Office, should first be read by him this was accepted by the Executive. John Holmes owed his job to Mac and Mac took full advantage of it. At the time there was a member of the Executive from the Durham Branch where the Secretary was named Stan Hall who was extremely well-read and I remember him saying to me that he would be President of the Union – not you Derek, he added, because I am cleverer than you, and Stan led the battle to augment the Advisory Committee to include myself so we now had an Advisory Committee checking the General Secretary's letters, who could visit London whenever they wished. When the next round of election to sub-committees arrived, I was elected to the Education, but decided to be nominated for the Advisory Committee which was an extra duty. It turned out that whereas Stan was much cleverer than I was, I was much more popular and I beat him easy. So McEnery and myself had carte blanche to attend at Head Office wherever we felt like it. After a while it was decided to add a Committee man so that we now had McEnery and three others. When Mac got ill I became the Chairman. Soon after as the Union Vice President I moved from Education to the Finance Committee. When the elections were over and we met in Langland, John Holmes and Bill Ollerton from Preston Acre Gate Labour and others insisted that I took the Chair of the Finance Committee, I protested that I was happy to retain the Advisory Committee chair whose work had now developed, but felt it would be difficult to override the new Union President Arthur Bates, as Mac had established almost a tradition for the President to chair Finance. They would have none of it, and insisted that I accepted the nomination of Chair of both Committees. When the elected Finance Committee assembled for the first time I was nominated and then there was a long pause while Arthur Bates waited for his name to be put forward, nobody was prepared to do it, not even his drinking partner Billie Ollerton. I found myself in the awkward position as the new Vice President, humiliating the new President, who told me he would never ever work with me. I refrained from arguing, he was bitterly despondent over Billie Ollerton.

The main instigator of my appointment to Chair the Finance was Alf Pointon who was the Engineer at a large hospital in Stoke-on-Trent, President of his Branch, member of the Finance Committee, highly regarded and esteemed by everyone, a heavy drinker who never showed any signs. It was Alf who more than anyone, insisted on these moves and my consolation at the time was that with everyone on my side especially the big guns I ought to be able to cope. The Finance Committee also included Colin

Hughes, Jack Johnson, Oliver Cotterill, very powerful men and I should have coped, but I didn't. Gradually the pressures built up and I sensed the Committee were beginning to doubt my ability to manage the role of Vice President whilst in dispute with the President. The advisory and financial work became more pressured and others almost certainly noticed deterioration in my nervous state. This was aggravated by the fact that I was aware that the three Branch Secretaries were discussing me and planning a coup. My chief supporter Alf Pointon never attended another meeting after the Langland decision as he became too ill and died. I don't believe that the plot to unsettle me was motivated by any nasty intentions. I would have preferred them to have spoken earlier and when eventually they did suggest my resignation I was not particularly hurt, but in fact I think they were right to do so, and there was in my mind, a sense of relief. Oliver Cotterill was elected in my place, he was the Secretary of the West Midlands and enjoyed the position he had achieved, although I became unhappy about his close relationship with the new General Secretary, Frank Morris. These two seemed to combine together to frustrate the democratic wishes of the Union.

Oliver and I felt that Frank Morris was too easily, influenced. In 1977 on the occasion of the Queen's Jubilee, unbeknown to me as Vice President, the Union was asked to award two Silver Jubilee Medals. Frank Morris and Oliver Cotterill actually were the only people privy to this information. They awarded the medals to Arthur Bates the President and Billie Ollerton the longest serving EC member. I agreed with the decision, but this was a classic example of those two bypassing the Union Executive who should have made the decision. I still was able to trust Oliver Cotterill, but after he retired as a Branch Secretary and quit the Union Executive I was informed of some of his nefarious activities, particularly in regard to commissions on goods sold through the Branch Office. Whilst he was active on the Union Executive I tended to include him in the higher assessment I had of people like Jack Johnson, and Colin Hughes who were the other two plotters whose ingenuity and ability were of the highest order. Jack Johnson's command of the English language and Colin Hughes ability in fiscal matters were invaluable to the Union which at the time in the seventies was especially vibrant.

Whilst Frank Morris was the General Secretary the Government set up a Royal Commission and the very week in which it published its report, including its condemnation of Morris it was announced in the Honours List that he had been awarded the CBE. It is very difficult to know for certain but Frank Morris worked very, very closely with the Co-operative Press. We had a massive contract with them as in addition to printing the Journal, the Annual Report, and any other official papers for voting and ballots; they were always represented at the Union social functions. It is almost certain that Frank Morris's award was recommended by the Co-operative Press.

The Co-operatives have for many years appeared to be able to successfully recommend persons for Honours including Knighthood's and Peerages. Whilst writing about the Honours awarded for voluntary public work, it is worth mentioning that the Union has not been very blessed in this department. R S Chapman, General Secretary for twenty years, received a CBE this almost certainly came from the Co-operative recommendation. When he was sixty he retired and started a new career as General Secretary of the Co-operative Printing Society. Frank Castle his successor was awarded an MBE and I have no idea of the source. Ted McEnery became a CBE, although I do not know for sure I believe that it was probably through a political connection.

One day at the Blackpool Conference a couple of days before the meeting, some members of the EC had entertained the Assistant Chief Registrar and his wife to dinner. After talking to Alec Wilson I was boasting about Jimmy Cook from Coventry and his four children, three of whom were PHD's and the fourth son held a scientific degree. I went on to guild the lily and was telling Alec about Colin Hughes and his four wonderful children when he suddenly interrupted me to enquire as to whether or not I would accept an Honour. It seemed that some Civil Servants had it in their power to do this. I was a little reluctant, as it seemed to me that any honour falling upon me and the Union should have included Gladys, but she would have none of that, and enjoyed the award as much as myself and the visit with Tommy to Buckingham Palace for the investiture.

I was elected President of the Union in June 1981 and assumed the position on 1st July. This was a by-election caused by the resignation of Arthur Bates and there was just six months to run before the bi-annual elections were to be held. I decided to use that time to consolidate my position and seek nomination in October and canvas for votes in November and December and then begin from January 1982 my first two year term in office as the Union's President. During that first six months I played my hand carefully and set out certain parameters of procedural practise which I intended to follow in later years. I was easy going and given to making a compromise too often and others said I didn't compromise enough. I always thought the truth was half-way between the two. About the end of September, two men who I admired very much and who were both very influential, namely Harry Drysdale Chairman of Northumberland and Jimmy Ramshaw Chairman of Durham who later resigned from the Executive to become Chairman of the Federation Brewery for many years, took me on one side to give me some advice which was, in their words, "Derek stop pulling your punches". Much as I admired their experience I felt they did not understand I was simply sparring and I would hit when I became ready. After the election results were announced about the middle of December, I began work on my plan for the Union, to commence in January 1982. I set out the broader outline of my thinking and after Christmas posted a copy to every member of the National Executive Committee so that they had time to consider all the suggestions, ready for the first meeting of the new Committee which was to be held at Broadstairs. The plan is set out below:

1.) Function, Powers, Responsibility of NEC Rule 14A

2.) To Carry out Objects Rule 2

Full power to do all things necessary Rule 14
NEC shall control all business carried on
NEC may appoint committees

3.) Duty to individual clubs, members of clubs, their wives and children rule

4.) Often frustrated by:-

a.) Enemies
b.) Ignorance
c.) Parochial self-interest

d.) Inefficiency in administration

We can combat a) and b) the better if we overcome c) and perfect d) for which we only have ourselves to blame. We talk, we think, we have ideas but all too often no action results, on occasion because impediments are put in our way.

5.) I suggested we start with five standing committees

i)	Finance, Stores and Staffing	5
ii)	Administrative, Legal and Advisory	7
iii)	Convalescent Homes	7
iv)	Education	7
v)	Recreation	7

These Committees to be elected. The President and Vice President may seek election to one and the one Committee to which they are elected may if they wish, seek to become Chairman.

The President and Vice President shall be ex-officio members of all other Standing Committee but shall not vote therein or take the Chair.

Standing Committees shall be limited to expenditure on "one-off" non-recurring items of five hundred pounds. Any items requiring more finance shall be referred to Finance Committee prior to being submitted to NEC. Standing Committees may appoint sub-committees to deal with matters relating to their specific duties, e.g. finance, stores and staff may appoint negotiators for Trade Union matters.

6.) I suggest the creation of ad hoc committees to be on the following basis:-

i). The NEC may instruct the President or the General Secretary to appoint an ad hoc committee of not more than four members plus the President and/or the General Secretary.

ii). No ad hoc to exist for more than six months from date of appointment.

iii) It may not incur expenditure other than a maximum of two hundred and fifty pounds for professional advice, without the prior consent of the NEC.

iv) It shall have access to all documents, letters files, records, accounts and any other information contained at Head Office or any Branch Office.

v) It shall have authority to meet any Standing Committee for purposes directly connected with its terms of reference.

vi) It shall report its findings in writing to the NEC, such reports to be in the hands of the NEC at least two weeks prior to discussion of its recommendations. It may make Progress Reports.

vii) It may meet at Head Office or elsewhere. There will be no Chairman and no formal procedures. Minority reports may be permitted.

viii) It may investigate the progress of any subject or issue which may have previously been resolved by the NEC.

ix) It shall, within its terms of reference during its period of activity, act under and on behalf of the authority of the NEC.

7.) Appointments to outside bodies, delegates, representatives, e.g. Catering (Non-Residential) Wages Council, Job Evaluation, Ruskin College, Workers Education Association, will be made by the full NEC. Standing Committees may make recommendations.

8.) Suggested list of subjects for consideration by ad hoc.

a.) Redefine the function and financing of Branches.
b.) Investigate the Statistical Returns from clubs, and redefine the data required.
c.) The valuation of all Union land – property – fixtures, fittings and equipment.
d.) Removal of Head Office from London.
e.) Establishment of a Public Relations Department Committee.
f.) Evaluation and extension of Branch Secretary's Conferences.
g.) National Elections – Assistance to candidates ref: Election Addresses – use of Branch Funds?

h.) Installation of a computer at Head Office
i.) Setting up of a Club Journal Board to work with the Editor and the Co-Op Press.
j.) Development of contact between the Union and the Clubs Breweries.
k.) Possibility of change from Barclays to Co-op Bank.
l.) Provision of office accommodation for President at Head Office.
m.) Development of unused area at Head Office.
n.) Protection of Branch Secretaries, security of employment – salaries pensions.
o.) Feasibility of Standing Committee meetings earlier to enable written reports of proceedings to be presented to NEC
p.) Enquire as to changing normal NEC meetings from Saturday to mid-week.

I was reasonably confident that the NEC would see the merit in the work I had prepared.

I was therefore shocked when at the meeting the plan was utterly and completely rejected. I later discovered that a scratch meeting of Finance Committee had been held on the Friday evening where it was decided to scupper the whole idea of these radical changes I had proposed.

Naturally I was very upset and I vented some of my temper on the way home on Saturday afternoon on Colin Wright who had driven Gladys and me to Broadstairs and back. It took me sometime to cool down and I immersed myself in the work of the Branch and that of controlling D J Dormer & Son Ltd, although by now Tommy and his wife Jeanette were contributing in that respect. I more or less decided that if the Union did not wish to modernise and go forward then it would be better to carry on as before and not create problems which always follow new innovations.

I therefore settled into an easy going attitude to the Union although in the back of my mind I was now looking forward to making my first Presidential address to the Blackpool Conference in April. However in March of that year Don McMahon of

Derbyshire telephoned to enquire as to what I was going to do about it and in my picque I said "nothing, do it yourself". So Don placed the matter on the agenda of the April meeting. There were some small modifications, but it was accepted.
Bearing in mind that the Conference had not really received an interesting address since the days of McEnery. Arthur Bates efforts were pathetic and almost an embarrassment. I decided to spend a great deal of time in preparation, in content, style, grammatical correctness and development and I looked forward with excitement. During this period I had at the same time withdrawn a little, I certainly was not punching again as the two men who advised me to take such a course were conspicuously absent from my corner at Broadstairs. Out of the blue came Don MacMahon with his suggestion to resurrect the plan and from April work began and I felt set on a Presidential career.

There were seventeen specific suggestions to be considered. All of them were given full attention and either implemented or tried and failed or rejected. There was one exception the first item on the list to redefine the function and financing of Branches has never really moved forward. A great deal of work has been done, stretching over several attempts and revived attempts to get agreement on these constitutional changes. Ideas were invited from right across the Union everything was considered all to no avail. Later Colin Hughes and myself with the help of Carol Goddard encamped in different hotels between Wales and London and drew up elaborate plans, all of these were rejected. In the late nineties the Union Working Party began again but to date have not produced an acceptable plan.

For many years there has been reluctance for the NEC to interfere with the structure or traditions of any individual branch. In the seventies the Union did form a Select Committee which considered the possibility of amalgamating branches into larger units. The members of that Committee were pilloried by others for daring to suggest any amalgamation, further the critics and opposition voiced their doubts as to whether the NEC had any power in this direction. My view always was and is that the NEC did have the power, this is emphasised in Rule 14 which grants full power to do all things necessary. Nevertheless the opposition was even more powerful. The only positive outcome of the Select Committee findings was the amalgamation at the time of the

Bucks Branch with the Northants & Beds which later became South East Midlands. In 1999 Jeff Lindsay from Huddersfield who had been a contender for the General Secretary-ship sought to take issue with the Union Executive on several matters. Jeffrey whom I admired and rated very highly had an almost impossible task in keeping the Huddersfield Branch viable. He represented both Huddersfield and Heavy Woollen for ten years or so until Colin Howroyd from Heavy Woollen defeated him. Jeff then had some foolish ideas about paying him a full time salary as a Branch Secretary in point of fact his Branch was by 1999 bankrupt. He recruited the assistance of the Trade Union which represents Head Office staff to demand a salary equivalent to that of the Union's Education Secretary.

One thing led to another, Jeff became alienated, the Branch in my own opinion was hardly functioning at all so I suggested to the Finance Committee that the Huddersfield Branch be closed down and the clubs transferred to Heavy Woollen for a minimum of two years. After that they would be allowed to apply for transfer to any other neighbouring Branch. The Finance Committee accepted the idea and put it to the NEC which went along with it, Kevin Smyth, Brian Winters and I discussed the matter with Jeff at Blackpool, he agreed that the Branch could not continue and arrangements were made for the transfer six months later. As we neared the date of reckoning, Jeff changed his attitude he then began an onslaught against the NEC claiming they had acted beyond their powers. He took the Union to the County Court in Huddersfield. The NEC briefed a Barrister and Jeffrey lost and this is what the Judge said, "I consider this to be a turning point in the history of the Union it clearly gives the Executive the power to close a Branch of the Union provided of course that there are good arguments for the action and the NEC does not act precipitously".

Rarely have people involved at management level in the CIU been prepared to enter into litigation against the Union. Jeff Lindsay was not the first, in my experience the first was Neil Robinson the then Assistant General Secretary. There is no doubt that in the main the classic club secretary up until about 1960 was the railway clerk or someone who worked in other jobs, for example town hall employees, men who worked in the office of coal mines and large and small industrial units. Often these people had some kind of secondary or grammar school education. They were the people who in the sixties and later graduated to positions at Branch level and ultimately National level.

There were one or two exceptions and I remember the President of Manchester Branch for reputedly fifty years until the mid fifties was a man by the name of KTS Dockray MA. There were several Branch officials with professional degrees. Gerald Classick was a Fellow Chartered Accountant and Treasurer of Manchester, Bert Rowe was another chartered accountant and Branch Secretary and NEC member for South Wales. Apart from these I knew of no-one who had any position in the Union with a professional or a university degree. Then about 1969 Colin Hughes took over from Bert Rowe and Colin had a BA from the University of Wales.

Colin had an immediate effect he was intellectual and certainly educationally head and shoulders above all of us on the Union Executive and all the staff employed in London. Most people held Colin in high esteem, his intelligence and abilities were well respected, some of course not least head office staff were somewhat fearful of his talents.
Then along came Neil Robinson to fill the vacancy of Assistant General Secretary. Neil had a third class law degree from Manchester University. Before long battles of wills began between Colin and Neil. These fights developed into embarrassing confrontations. So much so that at one stage on an occasion in Littlehampton they came very close to blows. I knew we could not much longer tolerate the presence of both at the same time.

I was well aware that Neil was inexperienced in club life and he certainly possessed the knack of getting under people's skin. Even so I believed that Colin could contribute far more to the Union in general and obviously South Wales in particular. The battle raged on and eventually Neil considered and decided to resign but not, I hasten to add, before he challenged the Union to an industrial tribunal held in London, on the grounds that we had acted unlawfully in not providing him with a Contract of Employment. Neil and his advisers worked out their case and Frank Morris created an answer. For some reason I was to be the main witness and naturally I practised with Frank Morris the statement I was to make. In the taxi ride we were going over the last minute practise when Frank Morris blurted out a question to me, he asked "can you remember the names of the other applicants on the occasion when we selected Neil Robinson" although that had happened about six or seven years earlier, I was able to tell him. This seemed to me to have nothing whatsoever to do with the case. When I took the stand and made my statement, Neil had the benefit of cross examining me, he endeavoured to prove that I could not possibly have remembered the things I had been saying, unless I had been prompted. To prove this at the climax of his examination he said to me, "can you remember the names of the other applicants when I was appointed", and I told him. I think the Chairman was impressed, little did he know we had been discussing it half-hour earlier. That was unlucky for Neil, but he didn't have much luck at all that day and he lost the appeal.

We were quickly down to one university graduate, but some years later I was delighted when David McDonald not exactly popular among the Union Executive, but he was an efficient Convalescent Homes Secretary, succeeded in obtaining a BA Degree from the Open University. In my book this was no mean achievement, the demise of the convalescent homes is no way due to David McDonald.

Soon after I left Wolverton in 1964, the Government announced under the New Towns Act that Northampton was to be designated a New Town and developed under a commission appointed by the Government in conjunction with the Borough Council. The New Towns Act gave considerable new power to the Borough and there was no doubt that the town itself was in need of modernisation. General Plans were drawn up and published in a somewhat vague format.

Extract from Advisory Committee Meeting 24th February 1966

A letter was read from D.J.Dormer regarding the proposals for designating a site for a large new town in North Buckinghamshire, which would cover an area of some seventy-seven thousand acres, and would eventually house a population of a quarter of a million. At present the Rt. Hon. Richard Crossman, OBE, MP the Minister of Housing and Local Government, was in consultations with local authorities on the proposed scheme, and would be visiting Wolverton in connection with the matter on 11th March.

Following lengthy discussion, it was resolved that a deputation consisting of the President, D. J. Dormer and the General Secretary meet the Minister, if possible prior to his visit to Wolverton, in order to bring to his attention the need for land within the proposed redevelopment area to be left vacant for the formation of clubs.

If was further resolved to place on record appreciation and thanks to Mr. Dormer for bringing this important new development to the attention of the Executive.

My request was for each area, the Corporation should reserve a site for development by the inhabitants themselves; mostly I argued they would seek to build there a social club or tennis courts or some other form of recreation. The Corporation were prepared to do this, on the understanding that the Union purchased the land from them in the first place, which was a ridiculous request.

At the same time the Government designated a number of towns to be developed under the New Towns Act, including in my own area Northampton and Peterborough in addition to Milton Keynes.

I felt it necessary to keep clubs informed of any developments and proposals. In order to do this I arranged for meetings to be held on various sites to which club committees were invited to receive progress reports and to enquire as to the latest situation. Obviously everyone was concerned to know what would be the effect of the proposals on their own particular club. These meetings were over-crowded especially in Northampton and there was great demand for information, I with one or two delegates had made representation to the Borough Council and we were listened to most sympathetically. The Chief Executive, whose name was Mr. Almond attended upon us and gave much information, he deputed his second in command, David Pilkington to bear our concerns in his mind at all times. Through this co-operation with the Town Hall I was able to inform the clubs of much more detail than was available from other sources, however, they were not satisfied.

In Northampton in particular the plan for the redevelopment of the Town Centre involved the possible removal of nine Working Men's Clubs. This was a serious issue and I called a meeting of the Officers of the nine clubs in order to create a policy in respect of compensation and rebuilding. The nine clubs involved were Northampton Working Men's Club, Friendly Society, Fanciers, Vocal & Instrumental, Semilong, British Railway, Trades & Labour, Twentieth Century and Ex-Servicemen's. Eight of these clubs appointed me to act on their behalf in negotiations with the New Towns Authority and Northampton Borough.

I produced a report which gave a resume of the situation of each of the nine clubs starting with the most critically likely to be affected. I promised that the Union would be there fighting every inch of the way for the safeguarding of our nine clubs.

The three most critical sites were those occupied by the Friendlies, Fanciers and Twentieth Century. Throughout the next year or so, with the help of Mr. James Milne, an architect who had much experience in building clubs, I conducted negotiations to ensure that these clubs when they were demolished were re-housed in temporary accommodation while a new building was erected at the Corporation's expense. It was also clear that according to the law the new club had to be within a quarter of a mile of the original building and the total cost was to borne by the Authority. Car Parks were not required as they did not have them on the original site.

In later years looking through the names of those nine clubs, bearing in mind each one except perhaps the Railway Club was surrounded by hundreds and thousands of little terraced workers houses, it is fascinating to realise so many interests were represented and men with similar pastimes would band together to form Working Men's Clubs each with specific objectives.

The most vociferous man at several of these meetings of the club committees was Eddie Davis. Eddie was President of the Twentieth Century, a man I greatly admired; in fact I was a little afraid of him. I had known him for sometime and he had the ability to be severe when attacking, after a while he decided to attack the Union for its inability to stop the development of Northampton. Incidentally he later changed to become Secretary of his club and continued until he was over ninety years of age in that capacity. However Eddie announced one day at a mass meeting that rather than wait for the Union, his club had gone it alone. They had, he said appointed a top firm, well-known in the district, of Estate Agents Valuers and Surveyors to act for them. This most respectable firm he said had advised him and his Committee that they should insist on compensation when the club was demolished, of not less than £25,000. Eddie was proud of bringing off this coup, in the event although it sounds boastful, I personally took on their case and the compensation package amounted to at least one million pounds, I stayed friends with Eddie until he died.

The work I had now undertaken to obtain compensation for these nine clubs was enormous. I had D.J. Dormer & Son Ltd to manage, Secretary of the Branch, Member of the Union Executive and Chairman of Education, it meant a great deal of reading in order to become conversant with the New Towns Legislation and most importantly with the Compensation Act. Much time was taken up in meetings with the Council and I was fortunate in the technical matters by the introduction into my life of James R. Milne.

One day in Blackpool at the Union AGM Gladys and I and the children were staying at the Stuart Hotel. Jack Johnson informed me a friend of his wished to entertain me and my family to dinner. I was most suspicious and decided not to accept. That evening coming down the stairs with my family we were confronted by Jack and Sylvia his wife, together with Jimmy Milne. James could be a charming man and I could not be in these circumstances any way ill mannered. We accepted his invitation and over dinner Jack Johnson explained how Jimmy had built and re-designed and re-built Working Men's Clubs in the North East. Jack felt that there would be work for Jimmy Milne to do in my area. I was sufficiently impressed to invite Jimmy to my office the following week and to be truthful I was, although I had not realised it, in desperate need of technical assistance. From then on I worked closely with James Milne. The first club to be demolished was the Fanciers. In seeking compensation I realised on reading the Law that we would to be considered under Rule Five or Rule Six. Under Rule Six all the Authority needed to do was to find other premises for the club which were suitable or could be converted, that was the preferred approach of the Council but it was not mine. I knew much as they tried I would be able to find objections to an alternative site. Under Rule Five the Council were obliged to provide a Freehold site capable of erecting a building of similar space and facilities.

The site had to be within quarter mile of the existing site, furthermore no car parking would be required unless there was car parking originally. The total cost of conveying the site to the club erecting the building, paying the architect, engineers, surveyors, clerk of works and so on and the lawyers was to be met by the Borough. If temporary accommodation was required the Council had to provide it free. It seemed to be that my best policy was to go along with the Council's suggestion of Rule Six but my plans were all based on Rule Five. The first club to go was the Fanciers, Jimmy Milne appointed one of his staff to do the design, it was a dreadful monstrosity he built for which he had some kind of Architectural award. The club committee invited a TV star to open the club. I was invited to sit on the stage with him and others. His terms were a taxi from London and back and four hundred pounds cash in hand from the one arm bandit - not my kind of man. Whilst this was going on the Friendlies club were in temporary accommodation and Jimmy himself designed and oversaw the erection of their new building. The local paper Chronicle and Echo news carried a story that the local Working Men's Clubs were being rebuilt costing millions of pounds of rate-payers money which was true. Somebody must have drawn this to the attention of the District Auditor and questions were asked in the paper and elsewhere, as to whether or not there had been collusion and malpractice between me and David Pilkington, the Deputy Chief Executive of Northampton Borough Council, one of the most decent men I had ever met. He later became Chief Executive in Basingstoke. I don't know how far the District Auditor investigated David. It must have been a shock to him, I well remember how they investigated me but it did not shock me, I shocked them. First they wanted to know if the Northampton Borough Council had yet paid my fee, I explained I didn't do it for a fee, I felt it was a duty, they did not believe this but it was true and subsequently the District Auditor insisted that I charged the Council the standard approved fee which in this case was well over one thousand pounds which was quite a sum of money in those days. This was an instance where the complainants and the wicked innuendoes actually cost them more than had they kept their mouth shut. The Friendlies Club was completed, my friend Colin Wright, was the Secretary and Member of the Union Executive. The club invited Neil Robinson to have the honour of declaring the building open. I was forced to charge the standard fee of well over one thousand pounds.

The Twentieth Century club was next, that took a long time because Eddie Davis was difficult to satisfy as regards the new site. Eventually it was built and I got my fee, the three clubs combined, although I do not know the exact figures because fees are not based on land values, the total cost would have been well in excess of three million. One thing escaped most people, when they demolished the clubs, they demolished the housing and the consequence of this was in less than thirty years each of the three clubs closed its doors. There were still six clubs to deal with, Northampton Working Men's Club, always proud, always special, did not appoint me to act for them. They went to a valuer in London, what they did not know was that the London valuer came to see me at the CIU Head Quarters for advice on how to deal with the Working Men's compensation which I gave for nothing. In the event that club did not move until 1998 when it was opened by Brian Winters, the Union Vice President.

The Trades club was in a fairly critical situation, I well remember one evening when the Committee wished to see me, explaining I had a meeting at eight o'clock the same evening in Coventry I agreed to see them at seven o'clock en-route. I saw them, allayed their fears somewhat, they were appreciative of my visit and reassurance. After I had left the Committee meeting they resolved to sack me as their stocktaker, needless to say I was a little hurt when I was prepared to do their compensation job for free. As it happened they did not move for nearly twenty years. The four clubs remaining in inner Northampton are the Vocal, Semilong, and the LMS, now known as the Railwaymen's all of which seem to manage reasonably well, plus the Ex-Servicemens's which struggles to survive.

The sequel to the re-siting of the Working Men's Club in Northampton was that in the mid nineties my son Thomas acted on behalf of the club for its ultimate sale which realised, strangely enough almost exactly one million pounds. The club relocated to a building close to the Ex-Servicemens's this move I believe will have the effect of causing the final demise of the Ex-Servicemen's. The Working Men's Club will also have a struggle to survive.

Because of the problem of teaching management the differences between Industrial and Provident Societies and Friendly Societies I had believed since the fifties that there was a desperate requirement for a Club's Act. After the formation of the All Party Parliamentary Group in 1983 I began to believe in the feasibility of securing a Clubs Act on the statue book. In June 1993 some ten years after its formation the Group officially launched a proposal for such an Act. The foreword written and signed by Lawrence Cunliffe the Labour Chairman, John Watts the Conservative Chairman and Alan Beith representing the Liberal Democrats and Joint Vice Chairman of the Group said in the final paragraph ."We do not underestimate the challenge of turning the Clubs Bill into the Clubs Act. However with the wholehearted commitment of the organised clubs movement and the All Party-Parliamentary Group, we believe that the objective, however ambitious, can be secured."

The bill as proposed set out the principles safeguarding the objectives for non-profit making members clubs. At the time there were registered in Britain some thirty thousand clubs who would benefit from such an Act. That number has greatly decreased and by the turn of the century was probably down to twenty-three or twenty-five thousand. One important clause in the Bill made clear that those clubs which did not confer absolute equality for women would not be able to register under the Act nor enjoy any of its benefits. The proposals also made clear that proprietary clubs would be expressly excluded, there was to be recognition of umbrella organisations such as the Union and the Association of Conservative Clubs. The question of a club's legal status would be clearly defined. Matters of taxation particularly the difficulty raised from sales to associates would be properly cleared up as would the question of discretionary rate relief. Several years after this event it emerged that the Co-Operative Societies both wholesale and retail were voicing dissatisfaction with the legislation, namely the I & P acts under which they operated. They therefore determined to float a proposal for a Co-Operative Act. For one hundred years the Co-Operative movement had financed its own political party. Under its sponsorship a few MP's represented the Co-Operative Societies in Parliament. They were closely aligned to the Labour Party and by 1945 they were labelled Labour and Co-Operative.

Effectively they were Labour MP's and through this direct representation in Westminster it was possible for the Co-Operative to exercise a fairly strong influence in Government circles. The Co-Operative Movement has for many years been successful in nominating persons for honours and even creating peerages in the Upper House. Some of these have been direct and others have been after serving in the Commons. The Co-Operatives therefore led by Lord Graham and Lord Taylor were confident that they would be able to get Government time for their Bill.

Actually the Government had reservations as it was all too aware, certainly in Whitehall, that the clubs had an equally good case. In the clubs lobby which by now consisted of around two hundred MPs and Peers there was a large sprinkling of Co-Operative MPs who understood the requirements of both sections. Some of these people Dennis Turner, Ken Purchase, Bruce Grocott were anxious to appease and act for everybody. Through I believe their influence, the official Co-Operative Lobby approached me suggesting a joint venture for legislation. I attended a function in the Cholmondeley Room at the House of Lords, attended also by it seemed all of one hundred folk from all parts of the Co-Operative Movement. It indicated that I was quite happy because it seemed sensible that the clubs and Co-Operative should go in unison towards their goals. When certain members of the Co-Operative section discovered that some clubs did not allow ladies equality in membership, they were appalled, our tacit agreement to work together was conveniently dropped.

Whitehall would have none of it, and it was made clear that without the clubs co-operation the Co-Operatives could not process their Bill. This was desperate, the fact that the Co-Operative Bill had had a first reading which had been moved by Ken Purchase in what I would describe as a brilliant speech in the Chamber of the Commons. Still Whitehall would not budge and for that matter neither would the Prime Minister. Under Lord Graham the Co-Operatives continued their campaign which now included an attempt to persuade the CIU to withdraw its objections. A meeting was fixed early one evening with the Minister from the

Treasury Patricia Hewitt and her advisors, prior to this meeting I, together with Kevin Smyth and Norman Pritchard-Woollett were asked to meet Lord Graham with his Advisors from the Co-Operative Union. We met in another part of the Commons in a room especially booked by Lord Graham and there we were asked to withdraw from our objective for clubs, no threats or nasty remarks were made, but I was astonished that Lord Graham would be so naive and out of touch, he said it was essential we withdraw in order for him to have a clear field when we all met the Minister in one hours time. I am not sure, but I believe Kevin would have considered it I made it crystal clear that we would not. Lord Graham was devastated. I certainly did not wish to have a difference with the Co-Operatives but my duty was clear. We then were taken to meet with the Minister and her advisors, Lord Graham explained that the clubs refused to withdraw and his party would not proceed with the clubs whilst sexual inequality persisted. I made it clear that the leadership of the CIU was committed and overwhelmingly in favour of sexual equality. I explained that the Sex Discrimination Act could be simply amended in the manner in which I had previously demonstrated to Brenda Prentice a Government Whip. The Minister said that she had spoken to the Prime Minister on this issue the day before, Tony Blair was definite that he would not agree to the amendment to the Sex Discrimination Act. In his view it seemed clubs would make the decision for themselves. As the Co-Operatives could not continue with us while this situation applied and Whitehall would not allow them to continue without us, a state of stalemate was established. I did not enjoy being on opposite sides against the Co-Operative Movement, my whole background is so tied to and dependent upon the Co-Operative ideal, just the same the clubs movement must stay vigilant and when the Co-Operatives try again as they surely will, we must state our claim for our own Bill or at least part of theirs.

I have often wondered whether it would be in order for clubs to sponsor a few MPs as the Co-Operatives have done. It is a costly business and perhaps I should have spent more time in considering this move. As a boy in a great family, poor as church mice, proud as peacocks, loving but undemonstrative, forgiving and caring to talk around the meal table and around the fire centred on certain subjects, the Labour Party, Trade Unions, Co-Operative Movement, football, schools and with the exception of the ladies, Working Men's Clubs. As a young child the first two subjects were of little concern but the Co-Operative was most important. It seemed we had a motto, if the Co-Op didn't sell it, you didn't need it.

Every six months we looked forward to 'divi' day, in the days when three pounds ten shillings was a great weekly wage. My Mother would receive between ten and twelve pounds in cash from the Co-Operative and some vouchers to be spent in the Co-Operative shops. Many times when we required certain necessities in life, particularly clothes, we knew we had to wait for divi day. We were virtually banned from ever entering in shops other than the Co-operative. We lived at the back of, and above a Co-Operative Butchers shop, because of the size of the family I expect the Movement were sympathetic about the rent and rates. We owed much to this ideal and to this Movement. One of the serious misgivings in my life has been to see its decline. I had the privilege at one time of being a Director of my local Co-Operative Society this was quite a big business with a huge turnover in a large area of North bucks.

Whilst I was a Director of Wolverton Co-Operative Hugh Gatskell, then Leader of the Opposition was commissioned to produce a report setting out the way forward for the Movement and making recommendations. One of his suggestions was that Wolverton, Newport Pagnell and Bletchley amalgamated to provide Co-Operative services for the whole of North Bucks, this seemed a very sensible and practical idea. I welcomed it enthusiastically, it never got off the ground and I was defeated at the next election for the Board. Having left Wolverton and having developed a business based in computers I saw problems arising for the Co-Operative Movement in my new area. It seemed to me that much improvement could be achieved by amalgamation of certain functions. I thought that the dividend cheques were expensive to record and conceived a software programme to relieve local Co-Ops from this drudgery. I invited the Managing Secretary of the following Co-Ops to attend a meeting at my house, 50 Meadow Walk, Higham Ferrers to discuss the project. There were nine societies involved, they were Rushden, Higham Ferrers, Irchester, Finedon, Irthlingborough, Ringstead, Burton Latimer, Wellingborough and Kettering. They all turned up except Kettering, everyone agreed but as I suspected they were all clutching at straws, by then it was too late, most of these Societies were to go to the wall or to be taken over by the Co-Operative Retail Society Manchester. I still shop at the Co-Op.

In or about 1963/4 the Government announced there was to be a new City built in the North Buckinghamshire area. The initial plans obviously were drawn up in the modern concept, there were stories about an ultra modern monorail transport system, new industrial plants, decent housing for working people transferred mainly from London and leisure facilities. Although now living in Higham Ferrers I was delighted by these announcements and was well aware of the need for a better environment for working people to live and rear their families. Everything was to be done under the New Towns Act and the Government quickly moved to appoint a Chairman who was Lord Campbell of Erskine whose salary was five thousand pounds per year and the Managing Director of the New Development Corporation was a man named Ismay, whose salary was ten thousand pounds per year. My mind was already racing ahead, I had fears that the Corporation would bring in planners and academics who would carve up every inch of the land from Olney to Newport Pagnell, to Bletchley and beyond and round to Stony Stratford, Hanslope, Wolverton and New Bradwell. They would utilise every inch and I was aware they were under an obligation to make a profit by leasing the land they had acquired.

My view was that the community itself should be able to develop its own area after a settling in process. I had in mind people creating their own allotment areas, sporting facilities, children's play area and Working Men's Clubs. The City was to eventually consist of roughly two hundred and fifty thousand people divided into fifty groups of five thousand in other words fifty new small townships linked by a modern transport system. There is no doubt whatsoever that the planners have erected a fabulous City covering North Bucks. It is often referred to as the City of Trees and for my part I would find it difficult to make the slightest complaint concerning Milton Keynes, but in the early days I envisaged that with fifty new townships we would need fifty new Working Men's Clubs. Therefore even before Campbell and his men had appointed the Corporation, the Union invited Ismay to our new Head Office in Islington to come and discuss our views, he joined McEnery the President, Frank Castle, and myself. After an hour or so he made it clear there was no possibility of reserving any land for development by the population unless of course we were prepared to pay a rent to the Corporation for the land we wished to ultimately see developed by the people who lived nearby, my ambitions for Milton Keynes were dashed but we did not give in, there were already ten clubs within the designated area and we decided to endeavour to build forty more over the next twenty or thirty years. This process began by persuading Whitbread Brewery to obtain a site in Stacey Bushes just South of Wolverton. A Committee was formed at a meeting held at Wolverton Central Club, none of the indigenous population took part. Nevertheless a club was formed, a Committee appointed and the planning went ahead with the Brewery, the Development Corporation, the CIU and members. The Club Union were instrumental in helping with the rules and indeed in registering the Society with the Chief Registrar. Soon after the official opening of what was a beautiful club it became apparent to me that the clientele involved in managing had no intention of upholding the basic principles of club membership. I was soon informed they had no intention of joining the Union. They were capable, so they said of managing the club without any help, their concept of club life was entirely different. The Development Corporation took great delight, or some of them, in pointing out the failure of my basic idealism. I was bitterly disappointed, I had not understood the character of this influx of people, nor did I understand their standard of behaviour. The club quickly developed a dreadful reputation and went bankrupt. Many more attempts were made to recruit the community centre into the Union which had been set up by the Corporation. Much interest was shown as this would have provided a winning association, but there were all manner of difficulties and this also failed.

In the Thirties several experiments had been made in the most successful way in creating New Towns. Welwyn Garden City in Hertfordshire was probably one of the best examples. There were, of course, no Working Men's Clubs but when a large building which belonged to Marconi Wireless became surplus to their requirements, it was acquired after the war by the local Trades Council and Labour Party, who created a very successful Trades & Labour club in this building. Strangely enough quite close to Welwyn Garden City was Letchworth Garden City. This was a New Town created before the war and for some unknown reason no alcohol was allowed and even the one hotel did not provide alcoholic drink.

The Government had a long way to go, there were still hundreds and thousands of people in London who needed re-housing so the programme of creating new towns and developing old ones continued at a fast rate. In my own Branch I had Peterborough new town, Northampton new town, Daventry new town, Corby new town and Milton Keynes.

Ted McEnery, John Holmes and myself visited all these Corporations with the message but everywhere we were met by the demand to pay the rent of the land we required, perhaps for years before the club took shape. We formed several clubs which didn't have premises in Corby, Peterborough, Daventry and Northampton all of them fell apart for different reasons, but in too many cases there was the inability for the Committee to safeguard the small funds they had created. There was no doubt throughout the Sixties and early Seventies I learned with some dismay that the factors which bound the working class so closely together to do things for one another or the common good was beginning to show cracks. It was nobody's fault, our ideals and dreams of better environment still with the same industry, clubs, football teams, Co-Operative shops, Trade Unions and so on were being shattered. I personally spent a great deal of time in endeavouring to establish Working Men's Clubs where none existed, and it took me a long time to accept defeat. I have had earlier success in existing towns, mostly such as Towcester, Warmington, Leighton Buzzard, Farcet and various other areas, but new towns, although largely surviving often had a social problem as we had anticipated. For example, I recall when Telford New Town Development Corporation invited John Holmes and myself to discuss with them their particular social problem. It seemed the New Town having been established and several thousand of people already moved in, there was nowhere for them to go in the evenings. What had happened evidently so they explained, although they acquired the ownership of the land, a covenant was inserted in the deeds for vast tracks of land that no alcoholic beverages were to be even transported across it, excepting those of the local brewery, the consequence was the Corporation could not build any public houses. Their solution was to persuade the CIU to come along and build a series of Working Men's Clubs, this plan may have worked because clubs do not sell intoxicants, but the spoiling factor which prevented the plan taking place, was that the covenant clearly referred to the transport of alcohol. John Holmes and I came away from Telford somewhat disappointed, and I may say a little frustrated. Telford was left with the problem that every evening five or six double decker buses lined up in its town centre to take its population to nearby Wolverhampton where they enjoyed a social life and entertainment with a few drinks in the CIU clubs and elsewhere.

It is difficult for me to estimate how much time I have devoted over the years working with Development Corporations trying sometimes almost single handed, to establish clubs for people moving into new houses, new experiences with hardly any success whatsoever. At the same time I remain loyal to the concept of better working and living conditions for everybody. It would be no bad thing though it they were to generally help themselves a little more.

Club Breweries

Because of my deep seated belief in the Co-Operative Movement I was naturally drawn to the idea of clubs Co-Operative Breweries. In 1950 there were in existence some eight breweries owned and controlled by an elective committee of Working Men's Clubs. They were-

1.) Northern Clubs Federation
2.) York Clubs Brewery
3.) Preston Labour Clubs
4.) Lancaster Labour Clubs
5.) Walsall Labour Clubs
6.) Northants & Leicestershire
7.) South Wales & Monmouthshire
8.) Aylesford in Kent

I visited seven of these Breweries; Aylesford had already failed before I joined the NEC, now only one is in business that is the Northern Federation. The South Wales Brewery is now owned and controlled by one of the big brewery companies.

It seems to me strange that, in the days between the wars, when all of these breweries were established and the Union had between one thousand six hundred and two thousand eight hundred clubs they could begin these ventures and at that time operate them successfully. Yet after the Second World War, when clubs continued to grow to reach four thousand and thirty four by 1974 most of these breweries in that twenty-five years from 1939 had disappeared. This fact is also another commentary on the attitude of working people towards their collective assets. At the same time other factors were at work. In the late Fifties Bingo certainly changed the underlying attitude of club life more for the good I think, but the gaming machines which followed soon after the introduction of Bingo is far more questionable.

The Union Executive had certainly during my experience and probably from its inception held a strong anti-gambling stance. Scattered about the early Club Union literature are many references to the evils of gaming and undesirability of bookmakers. The early editions of 500 Points in Club Law deal with this activity in a strong and dismissive manner. So much as to say the Union held the view that few working people would be stupid enough to become addicted to the gambling habit.

Most gambling in any way was unlawful outside the race tracks. The Union dismissed bingo in one simple sentence in its 500 points, it simply said bingo, tombola or housey housey are unlawful. That was changed as I described earlier in the book by the action of Frank Castle.

The very thought of gaming machines or one armed bandits as they were called becoming available for play in Working Men's Clubs would have given rise to derision. In the early Fifties there were a few operators of a type of gaming machine worked somewhat as a toy. Although they tended to keep their activities confined to small isolated village clubs where they would not appear to be much of a threat they were specially frowned upon by Union officials locally and nationally. The machines themselves were inconspicuous.

So about the end of the Fifties the Government enacted a Bill to allow two gaming machines in most non-profit making members clubs. The machines themselves were mostly outdated, badly-worn imports from the USA and they paid a jackpot of five or six pounds for a sixpenny play.

At the first meeting after this announcement the Executive were in Eastbourne and every man expressed his horror and disbelief that any Government would permit these dreadful contraptions. The Union foresaw serious social problems arising, they saw members becoming addicted, families suffering, broken homes and general misery. It was therefore resolved that members of the Union would be advised not to install gaming facilities in clubs.

Both our insurers, Sun Alliance and Norman Frizzell, were informed that they were not to cover any matters arising from the introduction of these machines into clubs. It was also decided that under no circumstances would the Union offer or respond to pleas for legal advice concerning jackpot machines. The Executive undertook to fight to the last ditch any suggestion to the contrary. Branch Secretaries and Branch Executive Committees were similarly informed and called upon to resist this new innovation. In accordance with this policy in my capacity as Branch Secretary and EC Member, I used every opportunity to keep the status quo certainly in Northamptonshire, Bedfordshire and North Buckinghamshire. I was approached at one stage and informed that if I was prepared to stay quiet, there would be a payment to me personally of ten pounds for every machine installed. Eventually one club in my area gave way; it was Northampton Working Men's. This club has been established since about 1866, it stood in the middle of the town. It was successful and used virtually all day long. After a couple of weeks of one armed bandit activity the officials told me that their action had been taken reluctantly in view of the Union's feelings, but the Committee had decided to give gaming machines a trial. These two machines, it turned out between them, produced a net profit for the club of forty pounds per week. This was big money and when the news spread, I knew the battle was lost and almost overnight it seemed every club provided its members with this facility. It was easy money and there were many opportunities open to clubs to develop, to refurbish, to extend, to provide better facilities to keep beer cheap and in every way make clubs successful. On the down side apart from the damage to individuals, there grew up a spate of incidents concerning committee men and other club officers, being accused and indeed often found guilty of pilfering from these takings. Rumours abounded and the consequence of this was that many otherwise decent men with integrity felt they could not associate themselves with people or committees who were suspected or possibly proven to be thieves. A snowball effect developed quickly and instead of the competition to become elected to the management, clubs found that the nomination list at election times was often incomplete. Since that time things gradually worsened and it is now rare to have a battle to join the club management team.

There are of course other reasons which add to this problem. In the early days of the bandits when money seemed to be pouring in from the skies to the clubs coffers the brewery industry pricked up its ears, it concluded that this was where the money was. They set about investing in a huge way to make clubs bigger. Every day there seemed to be no limit to the amount of money a brewer would loan a club. Many clubs added large sections to their premises, but before long the bubble had burst.

Insufficient thought had been put into the added cost of bigger buildings, rates, heat and light, cleaning, maintenance, interest on the borrowed money, and shortage of committee men. Before long officials of clubs in many cases, began to rue the day of the legalisation of the one armed bandits. For the first ten or twelve years of this bonanza there was certainly an increase in the clubs' revenue. Nobody foresaw what was going to happen on the financial side in the long term.

In 1973 the Government introduced VAT. This law stated all forms of gambling were exempt from VAT. This led of course to the position whereby all clubs were partially exempt by virtue of the very large proportion of income which was attributable to gaming. The formula for determining the tax payable was complicated and very few Secretaries were able to complete the returns unaided. Worst was to come. After about two years of VAT the Government changed the law just slightly. It now read all forms of gaming are exempt from VAT excepting gaming machines. The Government had previously set about collecting some revenue from gaming by inventing a gaming machine licence duty. I would have thought that the licence duty was inflicted to make up for the fact that there was no VAT. When VAT was applied it might have been reasonable to suppose that the licence duty would be revoked. Not a bit of it – the very opposite applied and at frequent intervals thereafter, in some periods every year the Chancellor increased the gaming machine licence duty. Clubs who had enjoyed this introduction were now faced with the rent for the machines, the gaming machine licence duty of thirty pounds per week per machine, irrespective of the size of the club and VAT which started at ten percent dropped to eight percent went back to fifteen and then seventeen point five percent. All of which meant a smaller and smaller sum being paid into the clubs accounts. That was not the end of it, throughout the history of gaming machines there had been a tendency in some clubs to pay for certain class of work by skimming the money required from the top, and simply recording the balance. This practice was not particularly harmful to the club or the Government in the early days. After the introduction of VAT and where the habit continued, any money taken from the bandits as they were called to pay entertainers, cleaners or whatever was in fact defrauding Customs & Excise in addition to the Inland Revenue. The Revenue were not particularly concerned, but Customs & Excise were, and after some considerable study they were able to estimate the amount of takings shown on a balance sheet, as derived from the gaming machines and compare it as a percentage of the bar takings. Where gaming machine takings failed, often in a big way, to reach the percentage that Customs knew ought to register they then took a serious interest. Frequently they found over a period of three years that some clubs, had so contaminated their control, that the VAT payment frequently meant underpayment to Customs and Excise of thirty thousand pounds and more. I found it difficult to sympathise with clubs in this plight. During the Eighties I remember moving a motion as President, suggesting to the NEC that we ought to encourage the use of machines with meter readings. I suggested further that the meter readings and the actual machine takings should be posted weekly on the clubs notice board. The Union executive rejected the suggestion. This was a pity as by the turn of the century the metering of bandit takings had become very sophisticated.

The Union Executive had been knocked off its feet when we realised how popular the one armed bandit became. Although it must be recorded that again by the turn of the Century, the gaming machine industry believed that, only one member in twenty ever played the gaming machine in a club so the Executive changed its stance. John Holmes was now Secretary and he like others realised that the Union ought to have been in the market place. No revenue whatsoever accrued to the Union through this activity. We therefore determined that we would make the Union a national agent for the one armed bandits. This was a classic U-turn. We approached the main manufacturers, Bell Fruit in Nottingham. They were very interested in our proposal. Their Chief Executive and several assistants came to Head Office to discuss the arrangement. The idea being that the Union would be the agent and every club would rent these machines through us, they would be manufactured and serviced by Bell Fruit who were in the forefront of gaming machine technology. Their Chief Technician was a very capable man named Doctor Pilkington. Their number one public relations image was in the form of Brian Close, former cricket captain of England and Somerset, originally from Yorkshire. One day after a meeting in London it was particularly foggy, Brian was due in Derby for some kind of Broadcast; he said he was unsure of the route from our office to the M1. I volunteered to go with him, my car being at Wellingborough, but I would travel to Northampton, I was fascinated by the man and his conversation. The thing I remember most was the speed which he drove his sports type car along the M1 in the fog in the fast lane, hardly ever bothering to glance to the front. I hope I didn't show my fear then, but I freely admitted it later when we had a meeting in Nottingham. The trains had broken down and it was necessary to go to Leicester by road, I was the only one involved. Doctor Pilkington instructed Brian to take me by road from Nottingham to Leicester, and I declined. What Brian Close had revealed to me was the difference between ordinary mortals like me, and those of very highly fit individuals who could judge cricket balls, or whatever, travelling at vast speeds and treat them as they do. The deal was about to be signed, it was going to prove a very lucrative induction for the CIU, then the deal was off, it was off because virtually every other agent in Britain through their associations informed Bell Fruit that if they went ahead with the CIU deal, none of them would again sell Bell Fruit machines. On reflection I often wondered whether it was a form of poetic justice considering our original stance. I am not adverse to changing my mind in the light of new evidence or advice, but I do think that perhaps this was a change of ideal and perhaps we ought not to have done it.

The Union does of course now advise on insurance. We give advice and generally recognise the position of gaming machines in clubs. Strangely enough my view is still that perhaps we would be better in many ways without them. As I write this book just in the last week or two a Government appointed Review Body looking at gambling generally, has recommended that gaming machines should be removed from club premises. The idea is to replace them with machines for amusements only with small prizes. Naturally many clubs would find it difficult to survive without them. The Union is currently planning a campaign to counter the suggestion. During the next few months we will become very active in Parliament and throughout the country. I have no doubt that we shall win the debate and retain our gaming machines. All of this leaves one to ask the question what did clubs do in order to become established, to develop, to provide top class facilities, to be successful before the advent of bingo, totes and gaming machines. In the old days clubs probably had two raffles a year, the Derby sweep stake and the Christmas draw. Virtually all the money taken was returned to the players, for clubs never relied on gambling in any form to provide even a tiny amount of finance to support or maintain it.

Before becoming Secretary at Stony Stratford, I was once approached by the Chairman of Hanslope Working Men's who were seeking some improvement to their property. The club was housed in a former Public House owned by Northampton Brewery Company. The Committee applied to the Brewery for some improvement to the building, including the installation of toilet facilities. The only facilities that existed at the time was some twenty yards down the garden path, and men were obliged to hide themselves behind some corrugated iron sheets. For these dubious benefits the club paid an annual rent of fifty-two pounds to the Brewery. The Brewery Board, in a letter had stated in order for them to improve the building it would be necessary for the club to exercise more control over the bar and in addition the Brewery sought to increase the rent to one hundred and four pounds per year. The club Chairman, Bert Willingham sought my advice as to what the Committee should now do. When I examined the balance sheet I agreed with the Brewery that there needed to be considerable improvement in the bar stock control. I then wondered whether or not the Brewery could even after improving the premises raise the rent. Fortunately the club had a copy of the Tenancy Agreement dated around 1894. When I perused this document I noticed that in the first clause there was an option for the club instead of renting, to purchase the building and land for one thousand pounds. Hughie Gregory whom I knew as a member of the Bucks Branch Executive was shocked when I suggested that the club exercise this option.

Hughie had been aware of its existence, but considered that the raising of one thousand pounds was well beyond the capabilities of Hanslope club. Nevertheless, I persuaded the committee to take this route the club had about two hundred and fifty pounds to its credit in the Co-Operative Bank. Arrangements were made to borrow one thousand pounds from the bank, the building was conveyed to the club and I advised that nobody would be paid for any goods or services for six months. At the end of that time the club had wiped out its overdraft and Hughie Gregory who said he had not slept once in the six months period, was able to raise his head again after the shameful business of leaving bills unpaid. We became very firm friends until his death thirty years later. The club now belongs to its members, the Committee discovered new vigour and together with many volunteers, the club was virtually re-built, including indoor toilets connected to the main sewers for women as well as men. The staff were changed, the club prospered, the thatch was removed and replaced with tiles, the concert room was extended, the future of the club was assured. Hughie Gregory and I were made Honorary Life members. At about the same time I had information that Olney Working Men's were preparing to develop. This was before the arrival of gaming machines. Olney was led by a man named Jack Barnes who was articulate and capable. Jack always encouraged me in everything I did and I was anxious to help as much as possible. I cycled the ten miles to Olney to discuss with the committee ways and means of raising several thousands of pounds in order to bring about an extension of the club. The club previously decided to raise loans among the members. A loan certificate book had been printed and was ready for issuing the documents to members who were prepared to back the club. When I enquired as to the amount raised so far, Jack told me they had received two promises of five pounds. I resorted to my old well worn tactic of a bank overdraft, and holding up payments and the club developed on that basis. I am not especially proud of using that method and it certainly would not be allowed in today's commercial world, but I had learned these tricks working as a clerk in Lloyds Bank during the war. At the time of course I felt no guilt in any way. I was hell-bent at all times, to do what was necessary.

Sometimes the help I gave was of much less significance. I remember when seeking to qualify for a grant from Head Office to organise a skittles and cribbage league. I was one club short of the required numbers. I needed Newport Pagnell Working Men's Social to enter to make up the minimum number. The clubs fee to play in these leagues was ten shillings and they told me that could not afford to pay it. I therefore paid their entrance fee for both leagues; this amounted to one pound, which was equivalent to two weeks salary. I certainly did not feel guilty about that but I think the club did. In later years Newport Pagnell Social Club developed in a magnificent fashion and as for money, has been extremely successful. During the Forties whilst Leonard Allen was Secretary of the Branch there had been some scandal relating to the Secretary of Newport Club, his name was Jack Dunbabin, CMD. Jack was found guilty but appealed to the Union through arbitration and won his case. Even so he did not enjoy the continued suspicion which many men in the club world felt about him. I was warned when I became Secretary to watch out for Dunbabin. I was not prepared to condemn him because I knew nothing of his alleged misdemeanour. Jack Dunbabin was an extremely skilful man as a turner and worked on a lathe in Wolverton Works. I decided to get close to him and often sought his opinion and advice which was always forthcoming. He was anxious to re-establish himself in the club world and unfair though it may seem, he felt obliged it seemed to me, to want to clear his name a second time. This he did by becoming Vice President and the following year President of the Bucks Branch. The year after that he remained on the Executive Committee in the capacity of immediate past President, by then I had become a friend I thought, and I trusted him. One of the worst experiences I have ever had then occurred. The Branch needed some small printing job done, Jack undertook the task, he gave me a bill receipted which he had paid, I gave him the cash, one pound, eight shillings and sixpence, took the receipt then reimbursed myself through the Branch petty cash account. One day soon after in my absence, he persuaded the other members of the Branch Executive which included Hughie Gregory, Jim Reid the President of Bletchley and Fred Hewitt from Bradwell Progressive that I had claimed the one pound eight shilling and sixpence twice. He was clever enough to confuse these intelligent honest men that because there was a receipt showing the bill had been paid, I could not possibly claim it again through the petty cash. This was a most extraordinary trick and I was astonished that he would attempt this and it was obviously intended to destroy me as he had been almost destroyed himself. He went further and advised the Executive not to attend the next meeting as I was effectively condemned as a thief. Hughie Gregory told me of the plan. I in response hired a taxi, collected Fred Hewitt from Bradwell, Hughie from Hanslope and travelled to Bletchley to Jim Reid's club. The meeting had been convened to take place there and Dunbabin somehow learned of my action and with his own transport found his way quickly from Newport Pagnell to Bletchley. These four men were the Branch Executive Committee and when I explained the simplicity of the transaction which Dunbabin purported to be false, I became more and more distressed as I realised they still were finding some difficulty in believing such a simple truth. Dunbabin's action was devious, clever and vicious. He was enjoying the dilemma he had put me into. I believe in the end it was the friendship of Hughie Gregory that saved the day for me although I think Hughie was not entirely convinced of my innocence. I still have this receipt which Dunbabin had used in such a dreadful trick. It reminds me what a crook Dunbabin was and how right Len (Joey) Allen the Chief Reporter of the Wolverton Express was. If Dunbabin had been earlier wrongly accused I could possibly understand his need for revenge on someone, but now I believe he was almost certainly guilty. The whole episode was a great pity. I had no intention of allowing my name or that of my family, ever to be muddied by such wretched actions, and perhaps this was one reason why I was determined to establish a position in the Union for honour and integrity. Dunbabin had a successful business after leaving the railway as an automotive insurance assessor. He built up a credible business and often was very sympathetic to claims from club men motorists, but he was a crook. This was a pity as his children were very talented; his daughter was at school with my sister Eileen in the commercial college. One son went to the grammar school where I was, and very talented. One son became the Chief Executive, then known as the Clerk to the Newport Pagnell Rural District Council, a position of great responsibility which people esteemed and respected. One son a gentleman in every respect became understudy to his father and took on his business and yet their father was an out and out crook. Some people would say an evil man and I am one of them. His name should be expunged in any record of the Club

Union which conveyed any semblance of honour.

Work In Parliament and Reitrement

Historians of the Working Men's Club & Institute Union have written volumes about its original values. This includes the Reverend Henry Solly who had no concept of what working men really wanted. His idea of bringing them together under the supervision and guidance of the church, the local gentry and the mill owner who checked on their behaviour, whilst they drank their tea and oxo's was a long long way from the real ultimate goal. All the early attempts as most people know failed, and it was said by the historians, and I tend to agree with their assessment, that the reason for failure was the presence of the upper class, the presence of youth and the absence of alcohol. It was the great real leader, the man with real vision, Lord Roseberry and his friends, who realised that men wished to be given control of their own destiny, and when alcohol was allowed clubs began to thrive. Solly saw the errors of his ways and came back into the movement to guide it in its infancy. The Working Men's Club and Institute Union owes I think the most to Roseberry. It must have been difficult for the aristocracy for many of them to understand the kind of lives working people were leading, however much sympathy they may have had for the worker's difficulties. The pleasure, the excitement and the adventure of joining groups of men to provide for their own recreation, education and mental and moral improvement was extremely attractive. Then the greatest architect of all in building Working Men's Clubs arrived on the scene. This was B.T. Hall a great athlete and powerful speaker and it was said he had communist leanings, he was certainly a heavy drinker and he was very very capable. His writings I found, gave me much enthusiasm and guidance. There was a few years ago still in existence, a record made of B.T.Hall addressing a meeting of club men. I believe that he actually used Working Men's Clubs probably the first of many leaders to do so, this did not set a trend though because his assistant from about 1920 was R S Chapman CBE.

Chapman having survived the First World War where he was a medical orderly was employed in a legal practice somewhere in Monmouth and London. He was attracted to the job advertised by the Union and took up work with B.T. Hall until 1930 when he was elected General Secretary. I do not believe Chapman was a real clubman. He was very capable and he had strong connections with the Co-Operative movement. I remember attending a National Executive Committee meeting in 1950 when Chapman was still in office and he invited me to sit in the afternoon session that was a great privilege not permitted today. Chapman retired in 1951 at the Annual General Meeting of that year, this took place in the Pavilion at Brighton. McEnery who had not got on too well with Chapman during his five or six years of working together managed to degrade and certainly insult R S Chapman on the occasion of his retirement speech. I stood at the back of the hall close to one of Chapman's sons, a Doctor. As the moment neared for Chapman to make his final speech of farewell McEnery announced, to everybody's great surprise, that he was about to suspend the Conference whilst the Grand National was broadcast through the public address system. This took some three quarters of an hour, the meeting room was chaotic. The wonderful atmosphere that should have been created was destroyed. I felt disgusted; it was the second meeting I had attended. By the time Chapman made his speech, which is worth reading, the time was approaching six o'clock in the evening many delegates who were due to travel home became restless, and I wondered what it was that made men, otherwise great men, like McEnery want to be so ill-mannered and treat people in such a way. Chapman's assistant was a gentleman named Tom Nichol. Tom was a Londoner I think, not a clubman before he began his work with us. He did not want the promotion to General Secretary, he and I became very close friends and he used to spend his summer holidays or part of them at my house from where he went fishing every day. This he continued to do after his retirement whilst his health lasted. He had become somewhat frail during the last few working years. In those days it was compulsory for staff to retire at sixty. Chapman on reaching sixty took up the post of General Secretary to the Co-Operative Printing Society which he held I believe for about ten years. No females were employed at Club Union House then known as Club Union Buildings.

Incidentally I had quite a fight on my hands when the new offices were erected, to drop the word buildings, and call the new one Club Union House. It was a close run thing but I won that. Because Tommy Nichol did not seek the General Secretaryship there was to be a hard fought contest between two great club men for the first time. They were Albert Linsted CMD, the Secretary of South Yorkshire, member of the Executive and Finance Committee. A powerful debater and speaker fearless mentally and physically. An ex-miner, and ex-convict as a result of trade union activities, a man not to be trifled with he seemed to love me and somewhat unusually enjoyed preparing bullets for me to fire. But the other candidate was also a clubman. His credentials were somewhat different, he had been in the Royal Flying Corps in the 1st World War. He worked in a solicitors office and when he came to the Union he worked as the Legal Assistant. This job consisted of reading Hansard and Law Reports looking for references on any issue which may affect any matters involving clubs and licensed trade generally. Frank Castle won the election Albert Linstead fell out with the Yorkshire Council of Branches for failing to get sufficient support. McEnery was overjoyed because he had been unable to dominate Bob Chapman and he most certainly would not have dominated Albert Linstead, but he did dominate Frank Castle. Frank Castle became very popular, but he suffered immensely in private and at Union Executive meetings by McEnery who humiliated him at every opportunity. Frank was a clubman and a General Secretary who thoroughly understood them, very even tempered and displayed concern for his fellow men. Before Chapman retired he had complained that his work load was too heavy, this was owing to the fact that he had five Convalescent Homes to run and the service was becoming more popular by the day. The Union had advertised for an Assistant to perform the work relating to the homes although Chapman, as indeed Castle after him, always attended their meetings. The first Convalescent Homes Secretary was another partial club man, his name was Clifford Culling and he worked as a Co-Operative Insurance Society Representative in Bradford. I don't think he was essentially a club man but his work took him into this environment. He became immensely popular and with Chapman's and Castle's help raised huge sums of money for the Convalescent Homes.

On one occasion whilst at Langland with one of my colleagues, we were having a little innocent fun with one or two female staff, nothing nasty, nothing wrong, pure friendly banter. Clifford Culling took exception and made a serious threat to me, he said I am going to report you – I was not sure what he meant, to the Northants and Beds Committee who will have you removed from the Executive. "Well Clifford if they do I shall be missed more than you would be", I replied. Clifford retired soon after that.

After the Second World War Genard Ding returned from the war to recommence his employment as laid down by the Government. He had started work at fourteen and was not particularly well educated, having had six years in the Forces where he had become a Captain. He was an extremely good-looking man and he had energies and ideas for his job. It was a dual task being both Education and Recreation Secretary. Gen developed an air which led people to believe that he had a unique understanding and intelligence of every conceivable form of recreation and academic matters of education. He was certainly a good speaker and good organiser he also became extremely popular and I liked him, we got on well together although I never actually rated him very highly.

Most of this popularity which was created around people working in Head Office, was the use of continuous publicity in the Club Journal. Some of the reference to Head Office staff, and their brilliant handling of issues and organising, was in my opinion embarrassing. Up until this point we had no men working in London who had any family connection with the Working Men's Clubs and none of their own except Frank Castle. When John Holmes arrived for his interview for the Job of Legal Assistant he was offered the post. I was in the office in London and John did not have the bus fare home. We had a storekeeper named Bevan a very capable man who on learning of John Holmes' plight gave him two shillings and sixpence with which John brought ten players cigarettes and still left him enough for his bus fare. John never looked back, but if he had done, he would not have seen any Working Men's Clubs. On his promotion to Assistant General Secretary which he got in competition with me, the post of Legal Assistant went to a man named Arthur Spong. His father had a long history of Club life at Wolverton, he was a friend of my Father.

Arthur was certainly a member of the Wolverton Working Men's but he mainly used the Conservative Club in Bletchley. He had worked with me in Lloyds Bank in 1942. His illness kept him away from Military Service. After Arthur, we went for many years before we ever again employed another man who had any track record of membership in a Working Men's Club, there were a few exceptions after about 1980. It was because I was well aware of the pedigree of the power running the Union which I resented, that I became determined if I were ever in a position to do so, to ensure that if it was necessary to have semi-professionals administering the Union as seemed the case, then at least I could ensure that elected men from the grass roots who understood Clubs and Clubmen would at least control the Union and make their own mistakes. This is what I did. History will decide whether I am right or wrong.

Being President of the Union does provide quite a few opportunities to meet with famous people in all manner of activities. I suppose the most famous are the Royal Family and since 1955 I have had the rare opportunity of being a guest on four separate occasions at Royal Garden Parties, including my wife and daughter on the last occasion. There was also the occasion when I received the OBE when I was accompanied by Gladys and my son Tommy. Linda had been invited and was unable to join us as she had recently given birth. On that particular occasion the whole ceremony and the few moments I spoke with the Queen is recorded on an official film. There was another occasion when Tommy drove me into the Palace in my own car and his wife Jeanette recorded the moments on unofficial film which was quite a laugh. Another time I was asked to meet Princess Margaret as a result of the work the Union had recently organised, in connection with children's charities and particularly Great Ormond Street Children's Hospital. There have been a number of times over the years when in the position of Union President you are invited to events which are simultaneously attended by various members of the Royal Family, such as polo events in Great Windsor Park, Wimbledon and such like. I think the occasion which most impressed Gladys was when we were both asked to a ceremony in Westminster Abbey and Gladys' great thrill then, was to be sitting within a couple of yards of Princess Diana as she walked down the Aisle with Prince Charles, to take their seats in front.

Outside sporting and royalty most famous people I have met have been in politics. This is especially so in British politics and British Prime Ministers. The Speakers of the House whom I have been in conversation with included Horace King and the famous teetotaller George Thomas, Jack Wetherill, Betty Boothroyd and Michael Martin. I remember talking in 1955 with George Brown at a Buckingham Palace Garden Party. He had his two daughters with him and I rather warmed to them all. Later on I felt George became arrogant and somewhat out of his depth in the high position he found himself. On one occasion we were both invited to attend the annual dinner of the Corby Trades and Labour Club. There was some dispute or little misunderstanding about the order of speakers. It seemed to me that the sensible thing would be for me to perform the little official ceremony they asked me to do, and then for George to make his appeal. During the pre-dinner drinks I explained this to him and he said "Oh no I will speak first, these people have come here to listen to me, not you." This was a most ill-mannered comment, it was wrong, but he didn't get his way. Later on in life he made an absolute idiot of himself on a number of occasions as everybody knows. I always thought Harold Wilson was a martyr to tolerate George Brown as he did. I didn't actually speak to Harold Wilson, although I would like to have done so. I saw him on a number of occasions but that was all. Looking back and thinking of George Brown and his arrogance reminds me of the times I spent with Robert Maxwell, world renowned crook of the highest possible order, politician and perhaps the only real legitimate thing that ever happened to Maxwell was it seemed, there was no doubt, he was a hero in the field in Normandy.

My main interests were always the Co-Operative Movement, Trade Unions, Working Men's Clubs, gardening and football. To some degree local politics interested me. Around 1957 I was elected as a delegate representing the Wolverton Ward, to attend the selection meeting of the Labour party candidate for the Constituency Party in the Labour Hall at New Bradwell. A co-delegate with whom I sat was Mr. Donald Morgan who had been the Grammar School Headmaster since 1935 and carried on as such until the early Sixties. He had been a member of Wolverton District Council since about 1948. A very intelligent man and great teacher, he had read History at Cambridge. There were six candidates, each of them issued a written CV and each was allowed a short speech probably five or six minutes. Robert Maxwell was one of the candidates, and I well remember claimed in his address that he could speak six languages fluently. Donald

Morgan leaned over to me, in that case he said, he's not English, how true that turned out to be. There seemed no doubt that the six languages claim could be substantiated as could his Military Cross which the Tories subsequently tried to discredit. It was a pity, because there was so much more about Maxwell, had they taken the trouble, which they could have legitimately discredited. But then again we didn't know either. Donald Morgan, myself and others voted for Ray Bellchambers, a local man, well known decent family, absolute integrity and sincere. Strangely enough although Ray Bellchambers was a contentious objector during the war because of his good standing he was never pilloried for this. Just the same Ray did not receive the votes and Maxwell won the nomination. I have no doubt whatsoever in my mind, that the overriding factor which persuaded the long standing labour workers and party superiors, to vote for an unknown foreigner, was his display of wealth.

He was of course wealthy at that time having taken over the scientific publisher Pergamon Press and he was able through his flamboyant use of money during his campaign to become a member of Parliament. I must say that the Buckingham Constituency Labour Party were desperate for cash, in effect Maxwell purchased the seat. I could not wait for the election pending in 1959. When the time came, I took some time off from the Brewery, to travel with the Maxwell cavalcade, with his huge caravan and the enthusiasm flowed all around, the excitement was intense, he was fighting the sitting man, Sir Frank Markham, an ex Wolverton Grammar School boy from Stony Stratford, who had a long political career, and been a member of Parliament for three different parties.

Although he was branded a turncoat, I liked Frank Markham. Despite my passionate enthusiasm for the Labour Party I could never be rude to the opposition. I would claim that never once was I rude, discourteous or ill mannered. I still retain a great respect for MPs irrespective of party. Frank Markham recognised this and we had private talks. Frank Markham visited my house on several occasions, humble as it was. We did not talk politics, we talked solely about the Working Men's Clubs and Institute Union and I lent him a couple of books and uniquely in my experience he returned them when he had read them. I never had any sense of guilt or disloyalty because of my natural desire to speak to both sides and I became reasonably friendly with Maxwell and more than once Maxwell came to my little house in Anson Road where Gladys made cocoa and cheese sandwiches at ten and eleven o'clock at night while we talked politics.

Maxwell lost the election when it came in 1959, but he won next time in 1964 when Harold Wilson scored a great triumph. Wilson must have thought Maxwell was some kind of clown, even I was embarrassed when I learned that on his first day in the Commons, he actually sat on the front bench, as if Parliament had been waiting for him since it was built. His wealth did not impress Wilson or many others in the Wilson Government. To get him out of the way, somehow he was appointed Chairman of the Catering Committee, whereupon he sold all the best wines to make a profit. But he did not last in Parliament, he became so world famous as he lied his way through the newspaper world, and allowed his jealousy of Murdoch to take him down the criminal passages. It is sometimes forgotten that seven years before his dubious end, a report had been issued by the Department of Trade and Industry which unequivocally declared that Maxwell was not a fit person to be a Director of public company, yet despite that he was able to go on robbing ordinary people to the extent that he did. He must be the most infamous villain I have ever met.

Like most people I have been in the company of many men and women who have earned a position in the eyes of the nation which has made them household names. Very few of these have I been privileged to speak with. None of them would remember me anyhow, except perhaps the odd ones I have described. The Club and Institute Union has never thrown up great people who are recognised outside the Union itself, with one or two unusual exceptions. For instance, Hogson Pratt, a previous Union Secretary was once nominated for a Nobel Prize. Lord Rosebery, a previous President, became Prime Minister. One of the sixty or more Vice Presidents of the Union Sir Stafford Northcote became Chancellor of the Exchequer. Many of our former members in the sporting area became household names, having began their careers, or at least developed their careers, in the CIU. The most outstanding of these being Steve Davis of snooker fame, although we produced several others who became World Champion, or close to it and we certainly produced the World Amateur Billiards and Snooker Champion on more than one occasion. World Dart

Champions have been through the CIU programme and several continue to do so even after lifting the World Crown. Our Angling Champions on two occasions at least, have also concurrently held the World Angling Championship. These men are a credit not just to themselves, but to the CIU as well, and we have every right to be proud of them. I know little or nothing about their lives outside their sport, I do know a couple of anecdotes about Steve Davis.

On one occasion when travelling to lecture in Kent, I stopped off at a club in Plumstead for refreshments, and purely coincidentally Steve was playing an ordinary friendly game on the snooker table with one of his pals who I believe was Tony Meo. Steve Davis never ever won the CIU Billiard Championship but he came second once in a match staged at Wolverton Central Club. Prior to the match he was given a short technical lesson in billiards, by his opponent who beat him easily. Steve Davis never ever had any boastfulness about him, and I remember in 1987 when the Union celebrated its one hundred and twenty-five years we asked Steve if he would write a short article or message in our commemorative magazine, his reply was "write what you like and I will sign it."

At that time the Union made great effort to publicise itself for being one of the few working class institutions still operating after one hundred and twenty five years existence. The signs of change were already appearing and we were anxious to strengthen our base to instigate change, in order to face the future, and the next century. We had quite a few good ideas. One of them was to ask British Railways who had earlier introduced the 125 train if they would name one of the engines "The Club Union", they were shocked at the suggestion and said no, in any case, we had not said how much we would pay, not like Steve Davis! We didn't get an engine named after us, in some ways I am glad because it would have been rusted away and we are still going. But the 125 celebration did work in other ways. We set out to take the Union into the present and selected eight cities where a banquet would be held at intervals through the year, and each one would cover the surrounding branches. They were held in Newport, Northampton, Preston, Durham, Leeds, Leicester, Manchester and London. At each one there was a goodly representation of Parliament and local dignitaries. Towards the end of the year I personally became a little tired, as the pressure to keep up the momentum throughout the year was just a little too much. We made a film which cost a lot of money but which we had been promised would go out on one of the many TV channels. This never happened. The Producer would have been paid an extra thirty thousand pounds had he succeeded in broadcasting the film as promised. He was paid for the production, but he didn't get the extra. One day his father came to see me to tell me of his son's financial plight. I must have been a fool, and probably acted wrongly when I said we would pay him three thousand pounds now and the other twenty-seven thousand if he ever got the film shown. Which he didn't. I often felt that I spent three thousand without authority or justification I know I was motivated more by emotion than good sense.

We also produced a book called "Clubmen" this was written by George Tremlett. George Tremlett was first introduced to me about 1958 when I lived in Wolverton. He was a Coventry man, and became known to Pat Ansell who was the Warwickshire National Executive Committee representative. George had impressed himself on Pat with his literary ability, and as I was the initiator of the Centenary Committee, Pat thought he might be a good candidate to write a History of the Union's First Century. He made the effort to come and talk to me in Anson Road Wolverton and impressed me, which resulted in him being appointed the author of this important book. The book was well written in my view and is now quite rare. Later, George moved to London and although I was unaware of his existence in the political world, he made quite a name for himself politically. This was in the shape of being a Conservative member of the London County Council, which later became the Greater London Council. In 1987 therefore, he was easy to contact, and we asked George to compile the update, which was never as successful as the first one and are still easily obtainable. The Union lost a few thousand pounds in publishing this book, but for students of the CIU it is essential reading.

During one of the hundred and twenty five years celebration dinners held at Preston, I was introduced for the first time to Lawrence Cunliffe, MP for Leigh. Gladys was unable to accompany me and I joined with John Evans later Lord Evans, several other local MP's one or two wives, including Liz, the wife of Lawrence for the after-dinner dance. I enjoy dancing and took Liz onto the floor on several occasions.

Sitting around talking during the evening, I had experienced some reservations, although I was careful not to fracture any protocol, but I was most concerned that in the forthcoming vote in November, a couple of weeks away there would not be an unpleasant upset. The frontrunner for the Labour Party co-chairman of the Group was to be Roland Boyes. Roland was a man for whom I had a great deal of respect even admiration. He was especially friendly with Anne Clywd who seemed to be destined for higher office in any Labour administration. Roland who represented a Newcastle Upon Tyne seat, was naturally interested in the Club Group.

Anne was interested because of her South Wales connection, and more particularly because of her friendship with Roland. Carol Goddard and myself on several occasions made a foursome with them which I found very enlightening, and I was attracted to Anne whom I found a most delightful character and conversationalist. Despite all that I could not come to terms with the possibility of a teetotaller and vegetarian which Roland Boyes was, heading up our Clubs Group. I had had considerable help from Jack Dormand, later Lord Dormand, when the Group had been initiated, and he too was a teetotaller, and he was born in a Working Men's Club. None of this seemed to convince me that a teetotaller, despite his outward support, genuine though he was, could actually lead a group representing Working Men's Clubs. I knew I had no right to interfere with the election in Westminster. I knew I would have enjoyed Ann Clwyd's company perhaps more than Roland's. I knew my reason was based on thin ice.

When I tentatively made my point to John Evans and the rest of the MP's on the table, I was informed that Lawrence would make a great candidate. I did not really know him but I was getting on well with his wife. So the plan was made, the nominations were to be received by Lord Brooks, before mid-day the following Tuesday. Carol and I met Lawrence early that morning and gave his nomination into Lord Brooks just before mid-day. This was, incidentally, before we were granted passes into the house. Carol and I sat in the Central Lobby waiting to see someone at that time when Roland came in. We stood up to greet him and I said have you got your nomination in Roland, to which he answered yes. To my everlasting shame I did not inform him that we were aware of another nomination, and in any event it was a process from which officially Carol and I were excluded.

The election was to be the following Tuesday, Carol had the task of producing the ballot papers. Lord Brooks was the returning officer, only Labour members were entitled to vote. On a later occasion Peter Fry, Later Sir Peter Fry, my own MP, moved and carried a motion that all members of the Group, should be entitled to vote in all elections. On this occasion it was confined to Labour only. There were well over one hundred of them. Carol and I were close to the ballot box during the voting session.

Every single member of Parliament, from Durham and Northumberland and quite a lot form Yorkshire and it seemed to me with their friends from the Lords came to vote. Anne with her usual smile came up from South Wales to cast her vote. On the other hand Lawrence from 1979 to 1983 had been a Labour Whip for the North West. He was well known in Lancashire and Cheshire and he was an ex-miner. Therefore it was not going to be a walk over for Roland, in the event, Lawrence emerged the winner. Carol Goddard and I were saddened and yet somewhat relieved. Lawrence enjoyed the new profile he had obtained, not without some assistance from John Evans who not long after chaired the Labour Party Conference. Carol and I resolved to work closely with Lawrence Cunliffe, who became strongly dedicated to our cause. Although Lawrence was not a great Chairman or orator he relied a lot on his wife Liz, the group prospered more under his leadership than could be imagined. He did have a great deal of help from the Tory Chairman Greg Knight, and later John Watts, both of whom he seemed to be somewhat nervous of, but Lawrence had the knack and very highly tuned political skill to open doors. He used his experience as a Whip, he called in favours owed to him from that period, he arranged meetings with Ministers at every level. It seemed that any request we made to see any Minister, Lawrence would arrange within a few days. This included members of the Cabinet and there is not the slightest doubt that without Lawrence Cunliffe we would have not had a quarter of the success we enjoyed. Although I struggled with my conscious in Roland Boyes defeat which spoiled what could have been a great friendship with Anne Clwyd , as things turned out,

I am sure now that the decision was right because of Lawrence Cunliffe taking the interest he did, it was of incalculable benefit to our Union, every club in it and indeed every single member. In the Nineties Roland Boyes became ill and incapacitated. Anne lost favour with the powers in the Labour Party, Jack Brooks fell out with Lawrence but stayed on. Carol was unable to spare so much time from her family and I endeavoured to re-build the Group after the Labour landslide in 1997. Quite a few of the old Labour stalwarts moved to the Lords but remained members of the Group.

New members who took their seats in the Commons joined the Group, and although we lost a few Tories, the Group reached the two hundred mark and over during the Labour Government's first term. However there were not so many victories or successes, for us. Strangely enough the doors weren't so easy to open. I was not concerned as I resolved not to pressure this Government, realising they had so much on their plate to digest. My position has now changed. I appointed Kevin Smyth and Maxine Murphy to carry out the duties that Carol and I had done, Brian Winters and myself would be assisting as required. It did not work. Maxine certainly tried and she was officially appointed as Parliamentary Liaison Officer. Much as I have pressurised her to spend at least one evening a week in the House she seems unable to do it, Kevin does not encourage her, but whilst writing these pages I am re-doubling my efforts to force her hand. Out of sight and out of mind is a truism, but is more true in Westminster than anywhere I know. When Labour came to power there was a lull in the Group's activities, this was occasioned deliberately by me. In 1998 Nick Brown who had always been friendly towards me, addressed the CIU Conference at Blackpool, there he suggested to me that I ought to re-launch the Group with a party in the House. Throughout that Summer I had been unable to find a suitable room, then one evening in the bar drinking with Jack Brooks, Nick Brown who was the Government Chief Whip and lived at Number 12 Downing Street came in. Lord Brooks did not know him which surprised me, I introduced them and Jack being the Group's Secretary I quickly found an opening to say to Nick, I want to do a re-launch as you suggested, but I cannot find the accommodation. Nick said use Number 12. I could not believe my ears – I hope it didn't show. So Maxine and I began to make arrangements for a re-launch of the Club Group from

Number 12 Downing Street.

I then set about making arrangements for this very important gathering at Number 12 Downing Street. I called a meeting of the Union's Parliamentary Committee on the 21st June 1998 at Head Office, and explained the arrangements for the Group re-launch which was to take place the following Wednesday 24th. At that time the Group had one hundred and sixty-one members. One hundred and twenty-one parliamentarians both existing and new members had accepted the invitation. Of these sixty-one were new MP's or non-members and at least sixty of them joined the Group. We set about obtaining more and more support and I had a target of two hundred to make the Group really influential. By the end of 1998 there were one hundred and ninety-one members in the Group. At this time there were a number of issues facing the Union which needed to be resolved. We were having problems with the Performing Rights Society in connection with their commission. We took up a dispute with the Co-operative Bank arguing that they were not as favourable to Working Men's Clubs as we expected them to be. Early on in February of that year we were faced with a question as to whether or not when an Associate spent money in a club he was visiting that that transaction might well attract profits tax as it was not in the same regard as mutual trading. The Union appointed a Queens Counsel to give his opinion as regards the legality of the Associate ship and this he did on the 3rd June. His name was Michael Kent QC and his opinion was not as clear cut as the National Executive would have preferred, although the original dispensation was handed to the Union by the Chancellor of the Exchequer in May 1875. By the end of the year the Chief Registrar of Friendlies Societies, Miss Rosalind Gilmour was working on the proposals for the development of mutual societies. She and I worked very well together and I felt that she did appreciate very much the work the CIU was doing in this respect, and I had a strong feeling that she trusted me and relied on my opinions to a very large extent.

On reflection I feel that I ought to have taken the opportunity whilst Rosalind was still in office to seek some clear cut Act of Parliament to eliminate any doubt that Associate members of any club organisation could use other member clubs without contravening licensing law providing the individual club regulations permitted such activity.

In the years since I retired from any official position I have noticed that the regard to the law is becoming less and less.

By 1997 the All Parliamentary Group in the interests of clubs was operating very successfully. I was beginning to enjoy visiting Westminster regularly and I began to feel that my presence was useful for our movement and I did not feel a nuisance in any way. I listened and avoided trying to demonstrate any cleverness. I did establish a considerable number of very sincere friends especially Lord Brooks of Tremorfa. He had worked for many years with James later Lord Callahan as his constituency secretary in Cardiff, which Callahan represented in Westminster. I was invited to have talks with James Callahan as he was anxious to satisfy himself about my bonafides before agreeing to his long-standing friend and colleague Lord Brooks becoming involved with my activities. It did not take Lord Callahan long to accept that I posed no danger in any way to either his or Lord Brooks reputation. It was of some understanding at the request of James Callahan who talked to me about it Jack was made Secretary of the Group and for that reason we did find it necessary to spend a great deal of time together. I was always fascinated with his very writing, understanding and involvement on the political scene when he had operated mainly in the Glamorgan area of South Wales, particularly Cardiff. Jack said to me one day that the Group was obviously very important to non profit making members clubs and he wished to avoid the CIU taking deputation to the House with a particular problem and then the following week a British Legion club or some other group of clubs might wish to raise the same issue. Jack therefore instructed me to form an all embracing organisation so that all matters would be discussed on a priority basis prior to being brought into the parliamentary scene. I understood the purpose of this and as a consequence called a meeting to which I invited the Association of Conservative clubs, National Union of Liberal clubs Labour clubs, the Royal British Legion and the Miners Institutions. The Group met firstly in Head Office and was very enthusiastic. One of the first decisions we were faced with was to determine a name of this grouping of club associations. The suggestion came which we adopted, from the National Union of Liberal clubs whose spokesman was very open and forthright and he suggested the name, "Committee of Registered Clubs Association" the anagram for which was CORCA.. I was not particularly happy with that, nevertheless the majority were and CORCA was well and truly established and whenever meetings were held with the Parliamentary Group, representatives of all the CORCA elements were invited and on occasions when I attended as the spokesman I always made it clear I was representing the whole of the clubs movement in Britain as far as possible.

In 1997 the Registrar of Friendly Societies was demonstrating the power of his department and warning clubs that they were to heed the Act and that penalties would be inflicted if clubs failed to conform in regard to submitting their Annual Returns and any other matters relating to the clubs rules. Further the Registry were determined and insisted that alterations made on forms submitted to the department were not adjusted by tippex. They ordered that all forms be made out correctly and clubs must be aware of this before submitting requests for rule changes.

With all this involvement and demonstrations by the authority of the Registry in 1997, it is remarkable to record that a couple of years later on the 1st December 2001 the Registry was closed down and its duties were transferred to the newly created Financial Services Authority, who have over the years virtually forgotten about Friendly Societies and Industrial & Provident Societies except to say that they would prefer there were no Friendly Societies and strongly recommend that existing ones should transfer to Industrial & Provident Societies although if they had the Registry takes very little interest in them.

By 1999 the Government had made a number of laws to change the way in which mutual societies were regulated. It was also pleasing to note that ladies rights were becoming more and more to the fore and the equality the females were beginning to enjoy was much appreciated. Diana McKinley was brought into the Union Head Office to develop the computerisation of the administration and this carried on, on a permanent basis. There were now some two hundred members of the All Party Parliamentary Group and I began to feel that we had a first-class representation for non-profit making member's clubs in Parliament.

Many arguments ensued as regards the rights of organisations spending in other clubs and whether or not this should be taxable. Rosalyn Gilmore the Registrar of the Friendlies Societies was on our side. At this time the Co-operative Bank indicated they wished to improve their relationship with the CIU and I was very much in favour and supported the idea. At the same time I was beginning to worry a little because I noticed that the attendance at the annual meeting of the Union was beginning to fall. To some extent this was due to the fact that a number of clubs were folding up and the Union itself was becoming smaller. At that time women had not yet been granted rights to purchase a pass card and move from club to club. This was attended to with the new equality law which was passed in September.

In this year of 1999 Tommy my son was made a Union lecturer and gave his first talk in Manchester and he became quite popular over the next few years.

In February 2000 the Co-operative Bank published a book regarding its lending to CIU clubs when the Government decided to produce a new Licensing Act soon after the turn of the Century. I was shocked to find that one of the proposals was to permit the Police into private members clubs without warning or any notice. They felt they should be allowed in as many as they wished in uniform at any time. As soon as I was aware of their plans to include such legislation in the proposed new licensing act I sought to speak to the Minister concerned and I did organise a meeting with him and two of his senior civil servants. We arranged to have a meal in the House and during the course of this meeting I did make it clear that the proposal was completely, absolutely and utterly unacceptable for Working Men's Clubs and any other private members organisations. I made the point that these private organisations were established in order for people of like minded ideas to get together for local purposes and games. The working men's club is regarded by many of its members as an extension of the home and it enables ordinary working people to enjoy the means of social intercourse, mutual helpfulness, mental and moral improvement and rational recreation. It does not require control and overseeing by the police authority. The Minister and his officials said they would give thought to my views. We met again a few weeks later and I was informed that they had not been persuaded by me to change the proposed clause in the Bill. I was most hurt and distressed, they were very insistent that the police should have their way. I took a very belligerent attitude to this and I made it clear that neither I nor my organisation, would accept this without a fight. As a consequence we met again two or three weeks later when the Minister informed me that they had finally accepted my view and the clause had been removed from the proposed licensing Bill. It seems that when the police discovered their suggestion of right of entry into private clubs had been removed they were inflamed and as far as I can understand it their officers visited the department to demand why their suggestion had been removed. I have no proof but I rather imagine that one of the civil servants without being malicious and not thinking mentioned my name and said I was not prepared to accept it. When the police discovered that I was the culprit for the removal of their request in the law change, I was then subjected to a continuous campaign to find me guilty of drink driving. For the next few months I was regularly stopped in many places, Bedford, Luton, Northampton, Wellingborough, Kettering and Rushden on all of the major roads at any time of night or day and breathalysed. I was even breathalysed in my kitchen, although I had invited them in as I did not wish my neighbours to see them breathalyse me. Needless to say I knew I would not test positive as I never consumed more than the legal limit and the continual pressure was beginning to have an effect upon me. I have also been extraordinarily pro-police and to be pursued in such a way was difficult for me to accept. Because of a misunderstanding with Jaguar I changed my car from them back to a Rover and as a consequence of this the police were not aware of my new registration number and the constant attempts to find me guilty of drunken driving ceased.

By now I had been serving the Union for 50 years, the last 30 as Vice President or President of the Union. I was beginning to feel the pressure being 74 years of age and I began to make plans for retirement at a suitable moment. All sorts of legislation and proposals were being talked about at this time. There were suggestions that clubs should be registered under the legislation in the same manner as Co-operative Societies or discussion ensued regarding ladies rights and equality. The Friendly Society was issuing new model rules. The Co-operative Bank expressed their wish to improve relations with the CIU and all its clubs. In 1997 the Union received a commission from the Performing Rights Society of £87,000.00. This was something I had worked for, for many years. By this time, around about the turn of the century, the attendance at the Union's Annual General Meetings began to fall. The Government had introduced breathalisation and the Union supported this law. The central investment fund of the Union had reached £1,712,000.00. The All Party Parliamentary Group which I had initiated was meeting regularly and successfully and kept its eye on any suggestion and new law effecting our movement. A new equality law was brought about, round about the turn of the century and this proved most successful.

In the year 2000 there was a suggestion in Parliament that the 1964 Licensing Act be reviewed, proposals were put forward in 2003, which included equal rights for men and women. The new Licensing Act was produced in the year 2003.

I am now in my nineties and looking back on my life which has principally been involved with Working Men's Clubs, I consider that I had a very happy and interesting career. I lived always with the advice of my mother ringing in my ears, never tell a lie and the policeman is always your friend. That last part came dangerously close to being a lie, when dozens of policemen used to pursue me in order to take a breath test in the hope of finding me guilty of drinking whilst driving, which they never did. I did not blame the individual policeman for having to carry this out, as they were under instruction of the senior officers who gave them their instructions, in order to breathalyse me.

When I finally retired from the CIU in 2010 from holding any official position in the Club Union, having been a Branch Secretary for some sixty years, several events and parties were held to thank me for the contributions I had made. I was delighted that the BBC East came and took a film in my office, a copy of which they gave to me to watch on my own television at home.

I was then proud of the speech made by the then Branch President, Mr. Barry Slasberg, and this is what he said.

"For 60 years Derek has been the father figure of the South East Midlands Branch and its predecessor. He has fought like a tiger when his clubs have been under threat. He has given comfort, help and advice when they have been troubled. He has educated when that has been needed and requested. He has also taken a real part in the social life of his own local club and others".

"Derek is the consummate clubman. Love him or loathe him, you cannot ignore the gargantuan contribution he has made to his Branch and beyond. This movement is in his blood and a good smattering of his blood is in this movement".

"Derek has truly earned a long, happy and healthy retirement, and that we wish him with both love and gratitude".

ND - #0103 - 080726 - C132 - 235/150/7 - PB - 9781784565640 - Gloss Lamination